How to Find Peace and Happiness in the Chaos of Everyday Life

ZEN for EVERYDAY LIFE

BY
MATT VALENTINE

Zen for Everyday Life

How to Find Peace and Happiness
in the Chaos of Everyday Life

By Matt Valentine

Buddhaimonia
ZEN FOR EVERYDAY LIFE

Buddhaimonia
ZEN FOR EVERYDAY LIFE

Table of Contents

Buddhaimonia
ZEN FOR EVERYDAY LIFE

Buddhaimonia
ZEN FOR EVERYDAY LIFE

Preface

Zen for Everyday Life serves as a universal path to transforming your stresses, difficulties, and suffering into peace, joy, and liberation.

I still remember the first time it happened. It was as if a boxer was using my heart as a speed bag. Bada'-bada'-bada'-bada'-bada'. My heart was practically beating out of my chest. My breathing became shallow. I didn't know it then, but what I had just experienced was the effect of heavy stress and anxiety. Over the next few months I would slowly begin to become aware of what was causing it.

First, there were the fears and worries that constantly ate at me. From my credit card debt, not having enough money to pay my rent, and having a new baby boy to care and provide for, to the fact that I was quickly approaching 30 and yet still hadn't come close to accomplishing anything of

Buddhaimonia
ZEN FOR EVERYDAY LIFE

value in my life. I had more to stress about than ever before.

Then there was the rushing around. An almost staple of modern life, I was further stressing myself out by rushing around in order to try and fix all of those problems which I was stressing about so that I wouldn't have to be stressed anymore. You can imagine I wasn't very successful! And when I wasn't trying to fix one of my problems, I was still rushing around. I was so used to it that I'd stress myself out over nothing.

Next, there was the deepest layer of the "self", where our demons live. It's the side of ourselves that most choose to ignore, to the point where many of us forget it even exists, but which has an unmistakably significant impact on our well-being. There was the fact that I was insecure about ever being wrong about anything, the fact that I hated the feeling of putting myself out there and being vulnerable, and the fact that I had never been shown the power or importance of caring for others, so I lived essentially for myself and my own selfish motives.

Later, I'd learn that the continued existence of all of these things, or rather the fact that they bothered me, essentially centered on the fact that I didn't have a spiritual or daily practice which in a way "maintained" my sense of inner peace. That is, a practice which deeply nourished my mind and

Buddhaimonia
ZEN FOR EVERYDAY LIFE

body on a regular basis and worked to unravel this negative self-talk. Sure, I ate well and exercised practically daily, that definitely helped, but I was under a lot of stress, had a lot of adversity, and a number of deep-seated issues that I needed to work out, and there was no amount of exercise that could help me overcome those things. What I really needed was to feed my mind and body, and work on myself, in a deeper way.

Finding a Better Way

My life changed when I discovered a little book by the name of *The Beginner's Guide to Zen Buddhism* by Jean Smith.

There wasn't anything particularly special about it, it was simply that: a beginner's guide to the practice of Zen Buddhism. It didn't really get into the meat of anything, it stayed on the surface level of Zen throughout the majority of the book and worked more as a gateway to further exploration (as intended), but, it explained everything **assuming the reader knew nothing about Zen.**

This was key. For someone who, at the time, had little knowledge of Buddhism, Zen, or any concept of spirituality for that matter, the very reason why the book was able to have such an

Buddhaimonia
ZEN FOR EVERYDAY LIFE

impact on me was that *it was in plain English.* Amazing concept, I know. So many books out there, not only on Zen or Buddhism but on spirituality in general, either use jargon (words the unintroduced reader won't understand), make the material too complicated, or speak in some other way that makes applying the material confusing. This can be OK, as some of it's necessary for higher levels of learning, but not for beginners, and therefore it's especially not suited for the new age of the internet where huge troves of people are becoming self-taught (or at least starting on their own). There needs to be a clearer path to learning for beginners which is accessible to everyone. A gateway, if you will, that gives people the opportunity to be properly introduced to a universal spiritual practice that nourishes one's mind and body and helps weed away at the negative self-talk that holds us back from finding peace and happiness.

This would eventually become one of my major reasons for writing *Zen for Everyday Life,* but it wasn't my only reason. My complete inspiration behind writing *Zen for Everyday Life* was to provide a convenient and universal resource to people which took the heart of Zen and presented it in a way that would help a person develop a daily practice that could bring peace and joy to their life *as it is,* and I wanted to explain it all

Buddhaimonia
ZEN FOR EVERYDAY LIFE

in simple, clear, and straightforward language in a way that made the material easy to implement from the time you take your eyes off the book.

By developing a daily practice that can bring peace and joy to your life *as it is*, I'm referring to finding peace right here in the present moment, without having to make any sort of significant life changes. This is a very important point. You need to understand that you're complete. You lack nothing. You're absolutely and completely whole. You're the Buddha, the very expression of your ultimate potential. You don't need to become something, gain something, or acquire something in order to find true peace and happiness. You need only to realize your own true nature right here in this moment.

The Buddhist path is, at its essence, simply about how to live life to the fullest. Those things which *all* of us are most concerned with: peace, happiness, and meaning. It's called Buddhism to notate those followers that live by the teachings of the original Buddha, it's not about worshipping the Buddha (who was a normal human being just like you and I), it's simply about living deeply in your everyday life in order to discover your true nature, and through that finding peace. Zen is the very expression of the Buddhist path fully realized in our everyday life. It's an experience, rather than a teaching. It's not a facial, a back massage, or a

Buddhaimonia
ZEN FOR EVERYDAY LIFE

serene feeling of calm. True Zen can't be put into words, only experienced in your everyday life. It's for this reason that you could say *Zen for Everyday Life* isn't Zen at all. It's about the *universal* principles which point *to* Zen and allow you to cultivate true peace and happiness in your everyday life. Let *Zen for Everyday Life* serve as a gateway to a deeper, more peaceful, and more meaningful existence. You can call it Zen, or you can call it not Zen. Whatever you decide to call it, it doesn't matter. What matters is that you realize the importance of developing a daily practice which nourishes your mind and body, and put that practice into action. And *Zen for Everyday Life* will show you how to do that.

A practice such as this is universal and transcends all labels and categorizations, and is where true Zen exists. It doesn't matter what religious affiliation you are, whether you consider yourself Christian, atheist, agnostic, simply spiritual, or something else altogether. It doesn't matter where you were born, or what race, age, or sex you are. *Zen for Everyday* Life serves as a universal path to transforming your stresses, difficulties, and suffering into peace, joy, and liberation. And the application of these principles is through practical techniques which you can easily and immediately begin to apply after reading.

Buddhaimonia
ZEN FOR EVERYDAY LIFE

The human race might seem very different from one another at times, but if you take a moment to look around you'll realize that we all have a lot in common. The greatest of which is our desire to relieve our pain and suffering and find peace and happiness, whether that's the desire for our own peace and happiness or the peace and happiness of others. This applies to the business owner who has hopes of making millions of dollars so that he can control his destiny, the man or woman searching for "the one" to complete themselves and start a family, the mother and father fighting to give their son or daughter a better life, the terrorist committing acts of violence on those he thinks are his enemies so that he can be rewarded in the afterlife with abundance, and the monk or nun sitting quietly in meditation. Take a moment to look around sometime, you might be surprised with what you find.

You can call it Zen, or you can call it not Zen. Whatever you call it, it doesn't matter. What matters is that you realize the importance of developing a daily practice which nourishes your mind and body, and put that practice into action. And Zen for Everyday Life will show you how to do that.

Buddhaimonia
ZEN FOR EVERYDAY LIFE

Introduction

Draw with your whole being.

"Want to draw with me, daddy?" My oldest son, who was two and a half at the time, said to me. "I'd love to draw with you baby, what do you want to draw with?" I said. He thought for a moment and then said, "mmm...crayons". So we took out a tin box of Crayola crayons and dumped them out on the floor.

We were sharing a large piece of paper some thirty inches wide by twenty inches tall. Despite all that white space, he generally liked to draw right on top of whatever I was drawing. If I went left, he followed, if I drew a circle, he'd draw over it. The best I could do was just continue to finish what I was drawing, because if I moved he'd just move with me. Naturally, I didn't mind, after all I was just drawing a random picture with some crayons. What was important was that I was spending time with my son, and it didn't matter how we did it. I

just made the best of it and simply enjoyed the experience of drawing with my son.

I can't recall how many times we've sat down to draw together, sometimes even using my Japanese style calligraphy set (I have to make sure he's pretty calm first, otherwise I'll end up with a room covered in black ink...), but this time something hit me. Call it a moment of insight if you will, whatever it was I realized something that day. I realized that life is a lot like drawing with my son.

What I mean by that is, there will always be *something*. *Something* will always be there, ready to cause you pain, suffering, or simply stress of some kind and ultimately get in the way of your peace and happiness. You're trying to get the kids ready for school, work on a project at work, cook dinner, or simply enjoy your off time, and *something* always wants to get in the way. *Something* is always trying to distract you *from the present moment*. When you're cooking dinner, that bill that's due next week is really where your mind is at. When you're supposed to be taking time off for yourself your mind is back at the office working on that project you have to finish. We live in an almost perpetual state of distraction and worry. Most of us don't notice it, but this has a profound effect on our overall well-being.

If you're waiting for the right climate to be happy, or think that if you take care of this one thing or get to this one point then you'll finally find peace, it will never happen. If you move out of your current house to a newer, bigger, and overall nicer home, you might think that you'll finally be happy. But after some time, the same issues, or different issues, will arise. *Something* always gets in the way. There's no running from it, and there's no hiding from it. But there is a solution.

Remember the realization I had when drawing with my son? All you have to do is...*keep drawing*. Don't go to another section of the page, don't go to another page, don't stop drawing, don't be distracted by the other crayons drawing around you, and most importantly *don't try to push the other crayon away. Draw with your whole being.* Be fully present for the drawing experience. Enjoy the moment for what it is, find the beauty in *this moment* instead of constantly looking elsewhere.

I hate to break it to you, but you won't find the peace you're searching for on a vacation in the Bahamas. That's only a shallow and temporary relief. You'll find peace in your own mind, in the heart of the chaos of your everyday life, and *Zen for Everyday Life* is about showing you how to do that. It's about showing you how you can find peace and happiness right now in this very moment. While walking to work, picking up the kids from basketball practice, cooking dinner, and amid all of your other regular everyday activities.

Buddhaimonia
ZEN FOR EVERYDAY LIFE

Living Zen

Zen for Everyday Life isn't about adding new things onto your life, it's about transforming your very life as it is into something altogether beautiful and joy-filled.

The word Zen translates directly as "meditation" in Japanese. When you look at the idea of meditation closely, what is it really? Especially in the Zen sense, it's simply doing an act with all of your being. When it comes right down to it, that's what Zen is- it's living your entire life with every ounce of your being and in every moment. By doing so fully you live expressing your own true nature without your critical or "little" mind getting in the way.

In Japan, particularly in the Soto school of Zen, this has primarily taken the form of zazen, which means literally "sitting/seated meditation" in Japanese. But Zen wasn't meant to be only about sitting in meditation, although this is a respectable path. In the words of Alan Watts, "there should also be a walking Zen, lying (down) Zen..." and so on. Therefore *Zen for Everyday Life* is about making your *entire* life into a meditation. But that doesn't just mean living with a gentle but complete

Buddhaimonia
ZEN FOR EVERYDAY LIFE

awareness of the present reality (mindfulness), it's also about learning how to live your entire life deeply, so as to see into the true nature of your life as a whole, discovering your true self and a great reverence for life that makes each moment fresh and beautiful.

Meditation isn't just sitting cross-legged on the floor with your eyes closed. You can practice meditation in so many different ways. *Zen for Everyday Life* will show you how you can use various forms of meditation and contemplation to transform the stresses, pains, and suffering of everyday life into inner peace, fortitude, and a great joy that pervades every moment of your life. I'll also cover a whole treasure trove of tips, tricks, and strategies which you can implement that will help enhance and support your practice.

Also, *Zen for Everyday Life* isn't just about throwing a bunch of things at you and letting you figure things out, or sort things out, for yourself. Look at it as the starter's guide to creating a daily practice of peace, or living Zen, where I'll guide you step-by-step through how to bring peace, joy, and overall *new life* to each of the most common (and otherwise mundane) activities in your daily life.

This is an important point that I'd like to touch on. Part of the reason why *Zen for Everyday Life* can help you find peace and happiness within your everyday life is because it literally transforms the very mundane everyday activities which you do each and every day (and largely take for granted) into opportunities for nourishing peace, healing, and joy. Therefore *Zen for Everyday Life* isn't about adding new things onto your life, it's about transforming your very life *as it is* into something altogether beautiful and joy-filled. It's literally *living Zen*.

And by a "daily practice of peace", I'm referring to learning how to deeply connect with yourself. That is, your *true* nature, not the guy or girl running around with 1,000 thoughts a minute, being controlled by impulses and desires (hint: that's not you). By daily practice, I'm referring to a set of daily activities and behaviors which encompass the act of touching your own true nature deeply, so as to discover and then maintain peace of mind, peace with those around you, and ultimately finding harmony with all living and nonliving beings. But as I mentioned, for the most part, these aren't exercises or techniques which are added onto your daily activities, more than that these are different ways of doing and perceiving the things that you already do repeatedly every single day.

Zen for Everyday Life, a Step-by Step System

You'll notice that each chapter in the book is either titled or starts with a verb. There's two reasons for this. First, I wanted to emphasize how important it is that you take action, so I made it as easy as possible to know exactly what typical everyday action you'll be working on for a particular chapter. From sitting, walking, creating, growing, and developing, to prioritizing, kindling, and planning, you'll know exactly what you'll be working on in each chapter. And second, because the book is about living Zen, each chapter is about capturing the Zen of each action, so the Walking chapter attempts to show you how to make your everyday walking into "walking Zen", and so on, transforming your life one common everyday action at a time.

Part I, *Finding Peace*, will introduce you to the most common misconceptions we develop about peace, happiness, and fulfillment in life as well as introduce you to the true path to peace and happiness through the two major tools of *Zen for Everyday Life*: meditation, the act of living grounded in the present moment with a clear and open awareness, and contemplation, the act of living and looking deeply at your life so as to see into the true nature of things, including yourself.

In Part II, *Being Peace*, and Part III, *Making Peace*, we'll cover over two dozen exercises using

Buddhaimonia
ZEN FOR EVERYDAY LIFE

both mindfulness and contemplation, as well as other techniques, to form a daily practice which brings peace and happiness to your daily life. And all of the practices we'll cover are about taking those things which you do on a daily basis and making *them* into meditations, not about going on some meditation retreat, or taking a trip to India to see the Bodhi tree (the tree Siddhārtha Gautama sat under before he attained enlightenment and became the Buddha).

Sure, those things *can* be valuable, and I'm not saying I don't look forward to taking a trip to India someday to see the original Bodhi tree of legend, but what's important is that you don't convince yourself that you need to make some sort of physical change or do something extraordinary for you to transform your life and find peace and happiness. Falling for this is falling for one of the major misconceptions I'll talk about in the next chapter (#6). If you can do that, then go and do that meditation retreat, it will be valuable and outside activities like that *do* help. But don't forget when you get back home that the change that needs to happen is *within*, not outside yourself, and you can do that no matter where you are. *That's* your focus, anything else is just there to enhance what you're already doing.

For those that want to take their practice further, support it, and help it grow Part IV,

Nurturing Peace, will do just that. Part IV is about developing a stable support system for your practice, and it covers five powerful strategies for nurturing and supporting your practice of peace and happiness. This is where your practice really begins to "expand", so to speak. Imagine this section as the building of a set of armor, each new chapter a new piece of armor. Each chapter in this section is meant to further enhance and support your overall practice and in many ways simply allow for many more opportunities to cultivate peace and gratitude in your everyday life.

Lastly, Part V rounds out *Zen for Everyday Life* by covering various important strategies and qualities for growing and maintaining your practice. There's more to a daily spiritual practice than the activity itself (after all, it doesn't just magically happen!)- there's establishing the activities as daily habits, developing the skills to support your practice, and, to some degree, finding better ways to manage your time if you lead even a marginally busy lifestyle, and Part V will cover all of that and more.

Remember that *Zen for Everyday Life* is about taking your life as it is right now and finding peace and happiness. You don't need to restructure your life in order to find peace, joy, or meaning in your life. But, keep in mind that some things might

have to change to take full advantage of your practice.

For instance, I'd suggest not running around like a crazy person half the day and actually convincing yourself that you're getting more done by rushing around so much (like I did). For the most part though, this will change naturally by adopting a practice that nourishes your mind and body as the one described in the following chapters. Also keep in mind, you might *want* to change some things. This is OK too, and can be highly beneficial. Just don't forget that if it's a changing of your physical surroundings, lifestyle, or anything such as that, it very well may contribute to or support your practice, but it's not the practice itself.

One last note: within these chapters are just examples of ways you can use these various practices. Look at each section as an important area to work on, and preferably get the hang of what's mentioned here before venturing out, but remember that once you do get the hang of things you *can* get creative in your own life and think of your own individual practices for, say, *Nurturing Peace (Part IV)*. Remember what's most important: to live mindfully and deeply aware of your interbeing and the precious nature of life in every moment. As long as your practice does that, you'll find peace.

Buddhaimonia
ZEN FOR EVERYDAY LIFE

Making the Most of *Zen for Everyday Life*

Before we get started, I'd like to lay some ground work. This book holds within it the keys to developing a daily practice which can help you transform your pain, suffering, and stresses into inner peace, true happiness, and total liberation. But this book in and of itself is just a collection of ideas, made into words, and placed onto a page. It can't think or act for you. So before continuing, I'd like us to make a deal.

First, you agree to take action on what I talk about in *Zen for Everyday Life*. That is, don't just read this book, say "Oh cool! That sounds great!", and then throw the book onto your shelf never to be seen again. Let's be honest with one another, you've probably done that before, maybe multiple times with other books. If you really want to change your life though, you need to take action, and there's no better time than now. Deal? Great. As my part of the deal I agree to make this book as simple, straightforward, and useful as possible. I also agree to make the meditations and exercises easy to apply in your own life from the moment you put the book down. So here it is again in detail, our deal together:

Your Commitment:

1. *I will take action on the information within this book.* This book ultimately doesn't have the ability to make you happy, bring you peace, or reduce your stress level. Only you can do that. Like the classic example of a finger pointing the way to the moon, this book isn't the moon, it can merely point the way. You can read this entire book tonight, turn around, throw it in your bookshelf, and never look at it again. It's just that easy. In order to create real change in your life you need to prioritize what it is that you want and take steps to achieve it. It won't happen unless you take action. Don't just read this book and move on. *Zen for Everyday Life* provides the steps, you just need to follow them and do the exercises.

In the proceeding chapters, I'll show you that peace and happiness are available to you in this very moment. Not in 10 years, or after that next promotion. Not after changing this or that, but in your everyday life as it is right now. But as I said, the pages of this book can't think, sit, walk, talk, or act for you. You need to be willing to take action and willing to make the commitment to find peace within. Both for yourself and for your family.

My Commitment:

1. I will make everything as simple, straightforward, and useful as possible. I promise not to throw a bunch of confusing information at you. Most importantly, there will be no use of jargon. If I use a word not commonly familiar to most people, I'll only do so when it improves the quality and usefulness of the text, and I promise to give a clear and thorough explanation of the word so that it doesn't affect your ability to absorb the content as a whole. My primary goal is to communicate the material of this book in a way that everyone can understand and apply. So I promise to keep things simple.

2. I will keep everything in universal terms. *Zen for Everyday Life* is for all people, not just those interested in Zen or Buddhism, and I promise to stick to that point throughout the book. This is a book meant simply to help you find peace and joy in your life *as it is*. It's a book about living each and every moment of your life to the fullest, and doing so in a way that

allows you to establish a foundation of peace and happiness for the rest of your life.

3. **I agree to give you everything I've got.** I agree to make this book as insanely useful as possible. This book covers literally dozens of useful techniques, tips, tricks, and strategies *all* of which I've used in my own life to go from stressed, anxious, and generally unsatisfied to a life filled with peace, joy, and freedom

> *You'll find peace and happiness within your own mind, in the heart of the chaos of your everyday life, and Zen for Everyday Life is about showing you how to do that.*

Buddhaimonia
ZEN FOR EVERYDAY LIFE

Part I: Finding Peace

Buddhaimonia
ZEN FOR EVERYDAY LIFE

Letting Go

Within you exists all the pieces necessary to lead a happy and peaceful life.

When I was younger, I'd always get money on my birthday. As a kid, naturally, I loved it. With money I could go to the toy store and pick out whatever I wanted, as opposed to getting gifts that I may or may not have wanted. Every year was the same, I'd end up with $100, maybe $200, and be free to use it for whatever I wanted. I still remember the feeling. At that age, there were few feelings as good as having a small wad of cash in my hand and the freedom to do with it what I pleased.

But something happened as I got older- the feeling began to fade. I suppose it was probably because I began noticing how fleeting the happiness I'd get from such situations was. Whatever the reason, I still remember what it felt like. I was just sitting there staring at the money

Buddhaimonia
ZEN FOR EVERYDAY LIFE

thinking "there's nothing I want to buy with this money", almost in a state of shock. I sat indefinitely thinking of what I might want to buy, almost in disbelief and with sadness at the fact that there was nothing I desired to buy with my money. But it didn't work. I couldn't think of anything. Money just didn't have the same effect on me anymore.

But what was probably the most memorable part of that experience was the feeling that followed after that: contentment. A subtle, but warm, feeling of contentment washed over me moments after my realization. I hadn't only realized that money no longer had the same effect on me, I had also realized in that moment that I didn't need money in order to be happy. I'm grateful to have had this realization at such a young age, and have carried it with me ever since.

When it comes to finding peace and happiness, essentially the overall aim in life for all people whether they realize it or not, there exists a number of major misconceptions. And these misconceptions can make us live our entire lives chasing illusions, running into dead ends, and ultimately suffering far more than is necessary.

We're convinced that in order to find peace and happiness we have to neglect our own well-being. Or rather, that if we do so we'll get there faster. But we believe this is OK, because once we

Buddhaimonia
ZEN FOR EVERYDAY LIFE

get there all of our problems will vanish and a state of perpetual happiness will have replaced it (happily ever after). But this couldn't be further from the truth.

What we really want is to find peace and happiness. But our idea about what that actually is, is wrong. Imagine you're climbing a mountain. You believe that on the other side of this mountain exists the happiness you're searching for. You believe that beyond all the headaches, beyond all the rushing around, and beyond all the sacrifices lies peace.

But you get to the other side of the mountain and...nothing. You look behind you and the mountain is gone. You turn back around and...there it is again- the mountain. It's then that you realize you're caught in a deadly cycle. This is the rat race. And it's what modern life has convinced us is the path to peace and happiness. But unfortunately, unlike this example, most of us never realize we're just spinning our wheels. These are just a few examples of the many misconceptions we've fallen for with regards to the path to true peace and happiness.

A Special Pair

Buddhaimonia
ZEN FOR EVERYDAY LIFE

As you of course know by now, *Zen for Everyday* Life is about helping you find peace and happiness amidst the chaos and craziness of your everyday life. But what I haven't explained yet is that this book is extremely actionable. *Zen for Everyday Life* is filled with steps you can take to create measurable results immediately from the moment you put the book down. Each and every chapter is filled with exercises meant to help you find greater peace, joy, and bring harmony to you in your everyday life even amidst all the usual craziness. And this chapter introduces the very first (and a very important) exercise.

I want you to imagine you're wearing a special pair of lenses. Have you seen those old flip lenses with the sunglass lenses that flip up to reveal eyeglass lenses? I want you to imagine you have a pair of those on, but a really special pair. How special? So special that you have as many as eleven colored lenses, one on top of another (quite a fashion statement). The purpose of this chapter is to begin the gradual process of lifting each one of those lenses, one after another, until you can see with perfect clarity.

What are these lenses? They're the various misconceptions that I just touched on, wrong perceptions about the way that the world works that hold you back from finding peace. Before you can become truly at peace you need to understand why you do what you do. Much of us operate on what's been deemed "common sense" by the collective consciousness. But a lot of this common sense is false and steers us in the wrong direction. This leads to us searching for peace and happiness where it does not exist. We've developed intricate myths and misconceptions that color our perception and make it impossible for us to see real peace and happiness even if it was staring us in the face. These are the various colored lenses which you wear over your eyes.

This chapter can be a lot to take in, so at the end I'll provide a full summary to recap everything we've covered. For now, the exercise is to do just two things:

1. First, simply let each misconception sit in your mind and don't try too hard to figure any of them out. Some of these might lead to sudden realizations, others will take time to realize. Think about them for a moment from time to time as you go about your day and see what thoughts naturally arise as a result of thinking about a particular misconception.

2. Second, as you go about your everyday life try to observe how these various misconceptions have affected what you do on a day-to-day basis. Go deep here, don't do yourself a disservice by staying on the surface level due to your ego or something else giving you some push-back.

These two exercises will allow you to slowly uncover the root of each misconception and to distance yourself from it, and the proceeding chapters will show you the true way to peace and happiness that sees through these many illusions. Whatever happens, approach them with a clear mind and have patience- the process of uncovering the truth can take time.

Letting Go of the Myth of Trading Time (and Ourselves) for Happiness

...by neglecting your well-being you're just postponing your own peace and happiness.

The first misconception is the myth that we need to neglect our well-being in the present in order to "get ahead" in life and ultimately *earn* happiness at some yet-undetermined date in the future. This idea is rampant in the modern world, where businessmen and women work long and

hard hours in order to make a better life for themselves and their loved ones.

But this effort is misguided. It won't result in you finding true peace or happiness because you're constantly chasing a dream and neglecting yourself in the present (and often, your loved ones as well). Any thought, and any idea, we have that we need to acquire something, become something, or do something special in order to find or earn happiness is misguided. Peace and happiness exist right here in this very moment, and any idea that either exists only as a result of you acquiring something you don't currently have, or that you need to earn it (rather- *feel you deserve it*) is a myth.

You don't have to give up a portion of your life, or yourself, to acquire the feeling that you're seeking. It doesn't exist in that life you're imagining, it exists in your own mind and can be felt in this very moment. If you acquired all of those things that you desire, you'd see that it doesn't bring you peace. Sure, you'd feel a bit better about yourself, and have some more peace of mind with regards to your finances, that counts for *something,* but it's not the true peace and happiness you imagine you'll acquire from achieving your goals. That only comes from turning inward to face yourself and realizing the beauty and significance of this moment.

But what if you're working for your children? I know how it feels, I'd do anything for my children. We're naturally inclined to want to give them a better life, as well as to neglect our own well-being in the process. For many of us, this is the most pure act of selflessness we'll experience in our entire lives. But you need to understand something very important:

Your efficiency, productivity, and overall performance in everything that you do is directly linked to your well-being.

Any idea that these things are separate is a misconception. When you walk, talk, type, think, organize, or strategize your mind and body work as one. It needs to put pieces together, shuffle things around so that it can look at things in new ways, and it needs to be free of mental clutter and obstacles in order to function at maximum creativity and efficiency. If you're working to improve your own life or the life of someone else you care about, take care of yourself.

More importantly though, by neglecting your well-being you're just postponing your own peace and happiness. You can be happy and at peace right here in this very moment and still work just as effectively towards your goals, so don't falsely convince yourself that you need to get

somewhere first before you can be happy. If you do that, you won't ever get to that "somewhere", it will stay off in the distance like a mirage in the desert. You won't know why you haven't reached it, because you keep "moving, moving, moving", but you won't. This can eventually lead to stress, frustration, a loss of hope, and altogether quitting on life.

We believe deep down that we need to earn peace and happiness, that otherwise we don't deserve it. Because of this, many of us actually keep ourselves from it on purpose without even realizing it. Don't believe the myth that you need to place aside your own well-being in order to find peace and happiness at the end of some imaginary rainbow. Big goals do take sacrifices, no one can argue with that, but they don't require you to sacrifice your peace and happiness. And anything that does isn't worth your time. The world can be a fast-moving place, don't lose sight of what's most important.

Letting Go of Past and Future

The present moment is life itself.

Buddhaimonia
ZEN FOR EVERYDAY LIFE

If you could step back and look at your life at a certain age and see everything that's held even the most minimal lasting effect on you, what you would see would disturb you. Ever seen an 8-layer dip? It's a dip made with various layers of salsa, guacamole, sour cream, melted cheese, among other things (and a dip I really, really like). Imagine that when you're looking at these various lasting effects which have built up within you from years of life conditioning that it appears in much the same way. Those times you were made fun of in high school represent a thin layer at the bottom, that difficult relationship from just a few years ago occupies a thick layer at the top, and all kinds of other past events, as well as social and overall life conditioning, fill in the middle area. Each of these events or constructs have contributed to conditioning you into the person you are today, and the total sum of this conditioning affects everything that you do.

But it's because of this very thing that we need to learn how to let go of the past and the future. The past tugs at us constantly, pushing and pulling us because of various fears and the negative self-talk that we've developed over the course of our lives. The future leaves us daydreaming, imagining things will end up much worse than they almost ever do and ultimately nudging us away from reality, the only place that peace truly exists.

The past and the future are illusions, figments of either our memory (past) or imagination (future). They're long gone memories, possibilities, or simply ideas never to be. It serves use to look back on the past and forward to the future in certain cases, but we should live grounded in the present moment. We exist solely in the present moment. *The present moment is life itself.* Live totally and completely present in each moment and you'll experience true peace by gradually releasing the bonds of fear and negative self-talk and gain a deep sense of meaning in your life beyond what words can describe.

Letting Go of the Fear of Facing Yourself

If it weren't for your stresses and difficulties, you wouldn't ever be able to find peace.

Well-being, from pain and suffering to peace and what we perceive to be happiness, exist simultaneously as two parts of one whole. There's no separating the two. It's because of your pain, suffering, and stresses that you're even able to find peace and happiness. If it weren't for your stresses and difficulties, you wouldn't ever be able to find

Buddhaimonia
ZEN FOR EVERYDAY LIFE

peace. There would be no peace to accomplish. You would be nothing but a blank white slate. In fact you couldn't even exist. There is no separating pain and peace, suffering and happiness, they are constantly playing at each other as the yin plays together with the yang.

So erase right now any idea that you need to, or can, run from your pain and suffering and lead any measurably peaceful life. It won't ever happen. In order to find peace we must first find out how to transform our pain and suffering. There's no other way, we can't find peace or happiness by ignoring our problems and trying to make lots of money, becoming successful, or acquiring false power. You'll find peace and happiness by finding the courage to face yourself.

Letting Go of the Mirage of Excitement

When life takes your breath away, breathe.

True happiness isn't excitement, excitement is fleeting and deceptive. Because it's such a strong positive emotion, when we feel excitement we tend to get carried away and think that everything is

Buddhaimonia
ZEN FOR EVERYDAY LIFE

great. Why should we be cautious of excitement? Because it's more akin to staring head-on into the headlights of a car than it is looking out from a window that gradually becomes clearer and clearer. You can get excited when experiencing the beauty of nature or you can get excited when going out to get drunk with friends, so excitement itself isn't any indicator of anything other than being in a high stimulus situation.

While excited, you're blind to everything else. Nothing has actually gotten better, or gone away. You're just in such a high emotional state that you don't notice anything else. There's nothing wrong with excitement in itself, but you need to be careful not to confuse it with true peace or happiness.

I'm not saying try not to be excited. Enjoy it, but exercise caution around it because it's a strong illusion that convinces you that you're happy, at peace, or have found a "right place" in your life when you actually haven't.

Again, enjoy excitement, just don't let it fool you. If you do this you can enjoy excitement while not being carried away by it.

Letting Go of the Idea of Everlasting Happiness

Buddhaimonia
ZEN FOR EVERYDAY LIFE

Peace and happiness must be maintained, and this is done with a daily practice that deeply touches reality and nourishes your mind and body.

Everything in life is impermanent, ever-changing, and peace and happiness are no exception. This is one of the most important points on this list. Most of us are so convinced that once the right circumstances align for us we'll be happy for the rest of our lives. A "happily ever after" syndrome brought on by movies, T.V. shows, and commercials over the past century, it's a very real misconception that many suffer from.

There is no magical goal you can achieve that will make you happy for the rest of your life. Peace and happiness must be maintained, and this is done with a daily practice that deeply touches reality and nourishes your mind and body. Develop a daily practice and follow it with diligence as a life-long pursuit. If you do this you'll be able to cultivate a strong and resilient sense of peace and joy for your entire life.

Letting Go of Wanting Something Outside of Ourselves (and the Idea That Happiness Exists Only in One Place)

Buddhaimonia
ZEN FOR EVERYDAY LIFE

...an integral part of our negative self-talk as a collective species is the idea that we're lacking something.

One of the single greatest misconceptions of all, and one that underlies many of the other misconceptions in this chapter, is the idea that happiness exists outside of ourselves.

The vast majority of people believe they need *something* outside of themselves to be happy. We think that we need to achieve, discover, or acquire something to be happy, but this couldn't be more off the mark. We do need certain things for our basic well-being: food, clean drinking water, shelter, and human interaction. But what we think we need to be happy aren't the basic necessities for human survival, those of us that have those things often take them for granted and think that we need more such as a big house, a fast car, lots of money, or power over other people. But none of these things will make us truly happy or bring any measure of peace to our lives.

What happens if we do get these things? They make us feel good for a short while, eventually losing their luster and bringing us back to where we started (or in a worse position). They force us into an infinite cycle of consumption just to keep ourselves feeling good. This isn't true

Buddhaimonia
ZEN FOR EVERYDAY LIFE

happiness at all, but an illusion developed from our collective consciousness (which includes all people in a society- the U.S. has a collective consciousness, Japan has a collective consciousness, your family is a collective consciousness on a smaller scale, and the internet has even developed its own global collective consciousness).

Whatever it is that we think we need, we think that we're incomplete because of it and therefore won't ever have a happy life until we get it. This is an unimaginably dangerous lie we tell ourselves because it makes us think that we're inadequate or lacking in some way. But this couldn't be further from the truth. We're born absolutely perfectly whole in every way, and this means that peace and happiness comes from within. Catch yourself thinking anything less than that and you've just witnessed your negative self-talk in action. And an integral part of our negative self-talk as a collective species is the idea that we're lacking *something*.

If you're yet unsure of just how you're going to find happiness without acquiring all those things which you've always desired or thought you needed, just hang tight. The entirety of *Zen for Everyday Life* is about showing you how to do just that.

Letting Go of the Idea That Happiness Is Different for Each of Us

...mindfulness in one's everyday life, living deeply in order to develop a reverence for life as well as a sense of gratitude that pervades everything that you do, and learning how to live in peace with others and help your relationships prosper are fundamental principles which apply to all people.

You hear it everywhere: "What is happiness to you?" sums it up. We know that not everyone enjoys doing what we like to do, but does that mean that true inner peace and happiness, the kind we all strive to find, is found differently for each of us as well? Those things which we enjoy doing, even passionately enjoy doing, will not bring us lasting peace and happiness by themselves. They're what, for the most part, you'll do with your life. And they'll bring you a great sense of joy, but doing what you love isn't enough. Within doing what you love you need to have the necessary "ingredients" for peace and happiness to blossom.

It's romantic, that is, the idea that happiness is different for each of us. It's also convenient and allows us the affordability of not having to answer

the tough questions like how to face our demons. And that's what this myth amounts to: another way to avoid ourselves and not have to step outside our comfort zone.

True inner peace is found in the same way for each of us. That doesn't mean though that there's only one path. *Zen for Everyday Life* by itself has more than 40 exercises which you can use to bring peace and happiness to your everyday life, and I don't expect you to use all of them. Depending on what you do in your everyday life certain exercises will work better for you than others. And some you'll just prefer over others. But the most important point is that the basic principles are always there- greater awareness in one's everyday life (mindfulness), living deeply in order to develop a reverence for life as well as a sense of gratitude that pervades everything that you do, and learning how to live in peace with others and help your relationships prosper. These are fundamental principles which apply to all people. It might look a little different on the surface, but what we want is one and the same. And how we get it ultimately comes down to the same principles (principles which you can test in your own life).

Letting Go of the Idea of Advantages and Disadvantages

Erase all concept of advantages and disadvantages, challenges and lucky breaks, and any other place you attempt to divide reality.

Everything in life is like a coin. That is, everything in life has two sides or aspects, a positive and negative aspect, and this includes literally everything- even qualities like intelligence, beauty, and anger and can even include conditions like depression. The two aspects are, in a way, one inseparable essence. Don't get down over having a perceived disadvantage, there is an advantage in it, you need only look closely. And appreciate, but be careful about, a perceived advantage as this comes with it proportionate disadvantages. There is no disadvantage or advantage, there is simply you expressing your true self, your infinite nature.

High intelligence? Be careful, you're apt to overthink things, live in your head too often, overcomplicate, and be quicker to judge others. Quick to anger? Anger has a silver lining in that it's the mind's way of alerting you to something you think is wrong, so use that insight to discover what wrong perceptions you have and change them. Do

Buddhaimonia
ZEN FOR EVERYDAY LIFE

you have depression? You have the ability to appreciate a deep practice such as what's described in *Zen for Everyday Life* far more than most people, and this deep appreciation can ultimately lead to a much stronger practice.

Erase all concept of advantages and disadvantages, challenges and lucky breaks, and any other place you attempt to divide reality. These are all illusions, what you should be concerned with is living fully in the present moment and completely accepting of whatever comes your way.

Letting Go of Happiness

Seek head-on to transform your pain and suffering and you'll begin a beautiful journey of self-discovery that leads to a pure sense of peace and simple joys that pervade everything you do.

What is inner peace and what relationship does it have to happiness? Think of inner peace as the prerequisite for true happiness. Peace is the state accomplished once one has reconciled, cured, or come to terms with all erroneous mental factors, erasing the false constructs that plague the mind and keep it from finding peace. Inner peace is a fortress for the mind. This is why it allows us to attain *true* happiness. The happiness acquired

from attaining inner peace is unaffected by outside circumstances.

What most of us really want *isn't* for everything to be exciting and bursting with pleasure every second of every hour. Sure, we all want some of that, but what most of us really want is just for those things which are perpetually bothering us to go away so that we can have room to breathe and live in peace and simple joys.

We think we want to make more money. What we really want though is to stop worrying about money, whether it's worrying if we'll be able to provide for ourselves and our children or not or being held back by not making enough. We want to stop being so stressed out all the time. We want to stop being angry at our parents, or our ex-husband or ex-wife or that person that wronged us. It's less about what we want and more about what we don't want.

Inner peace *is* the happiness we desire. Absolute peace is the cessation of our pain and suffering and pure contentment with the present state of your life (the present moment). Seek head-on to transform your pain and suffering and you'll begin a beautiful journey of self-discovery that leads to a pure sense of peace and simple joys that pervade everything you do.

Buddhaimonia
ZEN FOR EVERYDAY LIFE

Letting Go of the Idea That Life is a Dark and Dreary Mess

The information we absorb from T.V. and the internet skews our perception of the world.

Many of us believe, due to the conditioning we've received growing up, that life is nothing but dark and dreary. It's hard, tragic, and depressing, and there's no getting away from it all. But this couldn't be further from the truth. Just as with everything else, in life there's equal positive to negative. The information we absorb from T.V. (particularly the news) and the internet skews our perception of the world. Step away from it all and experience life for yourself deeply in order to find the beauty and joy that exist in it alongside the hard times and tragedies.

The idea of the dark and dreary existence also leads to us believe that happiness is just an unattainable idea. But peace and happiness are not unattainable ideas at all, they can be accomplished with the right effort and further maintained through practice.

This misconception, like the others, is created completely and totally in our minds. But this idea is perpetuated by the collective consciousness- the various levels of societies we live in starting all the way back with our immediate family and stretching out to the world at large. The nightly news in most places, and headlines online, are just a weird combination of depressing and cute. They don't really give us an accurate representation of what life is really like. But they do skew our perception, and that affects our experiences which ends up negatively affecting our entire life.

Let go of these negative influences and prioritize experiencing life purely for yourself. Put aside these assumptions and see what it means to live peacefully with your whole being.

Letting Go of the Myth That You're Incomplete

...you're absolutely and utterly perfect just as you are.

I touched on this earlier, but it's such an important point that it requires its own section. This is arguably the most important misconception to let go of in this entire chapter. Much, or all, of what holds us back exists within this very

misconception. That is, the idea that you're incomplete.

The myth of self-improvement exists within this point as well. Self-improvement will have you believe that you need to improve some aspect of yourself in order to have a happier life. But to accept this means to accept that you yourself at this very moment are lacking something. That you're altogether incomplete and undeserving of peace and happiness in this very moment. The thing is, it's a lie. And because it's a lie, it's the most dangerous of all the various myths and misconceptions we tell ourselves. Because this is a lie, it becomes an altogether unattainable goal, and we end up hitting our heads against a brick wall all our lives trying to figure out what we're lacking.

Stop believing that you're incomplete. Stop believing that you need something or that you need to improve something before you can have a truly happy life. *Within you exists all the pieces necessary to lead a happy and peaceful life.* Stop believing the negative self-talk that pervades every moment of your life.

Many times, simply contemplating this very fact can be life-changing. When was the last time you said to yourself, "I am complete, I lack nothing to be happy and at peace. I can be happy right now in this very moment"? Do that for a couple weeks and say it with enthusiasm and as much belief as

Buddhaimonia
ZEN FOR EVERYDAY LIFE

you can muster and you'll already begin to notice a difference. Decide now to stop thinking you're incomplete and realize that you're absolutely and utterly perfect just as you are.

Discovering the Truth (Summary)

We covered a lot of important points in this first chapter, so it would be a good idea if we took a moment to review each misconception. Use this section if you want to quickly review the 11 misconceptions:

1. Letting Go of the Myth of Trading Time (and Ourselves) for Happiness

By neglecting your well-being you're just postponing your own peace and happiness. You can be happy and at peace right here in this very moment and still work just as effectively towards your dreams and goals, so don't falsely convince yourself that you need to get somewhere first before you can be happy, or that you need to work to "deserve" happiness. You deserve happiness now just as you are.

Buddhaimonia
ZEN FOR EVERYDAY LIFE

2. Letting Go of Past and Future

The past and the future are illusions, figments of our imagination either long gone, possibilities, or simply ideas never to be. It serves us to look back on the past and forward to the future in certain cases, but we should live grounded in the present moment.

3. Letting Go of the Fear of Facing Yourself

Well-being, from pain and suffering to peace and what we perceive to be happiness, exist simultaneously as two parts of one whole. There's no separating the two. If it weren't for your stresses and difficulties, you wouldn't ever be able to find peace. You'll find peace and happiness by finding the courage to face yourself.

4. Letting Go of the Mirage of Excitement

True happiness isn't excitement, excitement is fleeting and deceptive. Enjoy it, but exercise caution around it.

5. Letting Go of the Idea of Everlasting Happiness

Everything in life is impermanent, ever-changing, and peace and happiness is included in that. Develop a daily practice and follow it with diligence. This is true peace.

6. Letting Go of Wanting Something Outside of Ourselves (and the Idea That Happiness Exists Only in One Place)

The vast majority of people believe they need *something* outside of themselves to be happy. We think we need more, more, and more- a big house, a fast car, lots of money, and power over other people. But none of these things will make us truly happy or bring any measure of peace to our lives because peace and happiness come from within.

Buddhaimonia
ZEN FOR EVERYDAY LIFE

7. Letting Go of the Idea That Happiness is Different for Each of Us

It might look a little different on the surface, but what we want is one in the same. And how we get it ultimately comes down to the same principles (principles which you can test in your own life).

8. Letting Go of the Idea of Advantages and Disadvantages

Erase all concept of advantages and disadvantages, challenges and lucky breaks, and any other place you attempt to divide reality. These are all illusions, what you should be concerned with is living fully in the present moment and fully accepting of whatever comes your way.

9. Letting Go of Happiness

Inner peace *is* the happiness most of us desire. Absolute peace is the cessation of our pain and suffering and pure contentment with the present state of your life (the present moment). Seek head-on to transform your pain and suffering and you'll begin a beautiful journey of self-discovery that leads to a pure sense of peace and simple joys that pervade everything you do.

10. Letting Go of the Idea That Life is a Dark and Dreary Mess

Many of us believe that life is nothing but dark and dreary. This couldn't be further from the truth. Just as with everything else, in life there's equal positive to negative. Experience life purely for yourself and you'll find an equal amount of peace and joy to be had.

11. Letting Go of the Myth That You're Incomplete

Self-improvement will have you believe that you need to improve some aspect of yourself in order to have a happier life. But to accept this means to accept that you yourself at this very moment are lacking something. This is a lie. Stop believing that you're incomplete. *Within you exist all the pieces necessary to lead a happy and peaceful life.*

Waking Up

There is no yesterday and no tomorrow, only the peace of the present moment.

Growing up, I felt as if I was living perpetually half-asleep. It's hard to describe, but I felt like I was never *really* fully awake. I was always watching myself. I felt detached in a general sense, and really had no idea why. At certain points, I thought that something might have been wrong with me. But looking back, from childhood all the way up to adulthood I was a deep thinker with a wild imagination and often lived in my head for what sometimes felt like days at a time. So while this was the major reason for my feeling detached from my daily life, it would, oddly enough, later help me identify and understand the major cause of our stress, unhappiness, and general feeling of unsatisfactoriness with life.

Imagine a dirty window. Through years of conditioning this window has amassed dirt and debris and is now almost completely covered from corner to corner. You can still see out of the window, it's still a functioning window, but just barely. This window is your awareness, and the dirt is all those things pulling you away from the present reality: regrets and reflections of the past, worries and occupations of the future, and general imagination filling in the gaps. Without even trying we end up this way by adulthood. From the strain of the past, to trying to control the future, to the influence of society on our thoughts and beliefs, and general recurring fantasies about life, this is a largely unstoppable process.

And it's because of our dirty window that we can live our entire lives without being able to see what's right in front of us. That is, the way to peace and happiness. But by cleaning our window we gain clarity and can see into the true nature of things, including ourselves.

How do we clean our window so that we can experience this pure state of peace and joy? With greater awareness, or "mindfulness". A level of awareness above that of simple consciousness, mindfulness is the act of becoming fully awake to the present moment or present reality. And training to live with mindfulness is like taking a washcloth to the window of your perception, as this greater level of awareness will bring clarity to your once clouded vision. Mindfulness is a pure, unobstructed, and ultimately complete focus on the present moment experience, with a gentle nudge towards what the central present moment experience is (your breath, steps, etc.). What I mean by that is, if you're drinking tea then in any given moment the central experience, your focus, could be the actual drinking and swallowing of the tea, the raising and lowering of your cup, the smelling of the tea, your breathing, or a loud external distraction. To make something a meditation with the use of mindfulness is simply to predetermine the area or pattern of concentration, or particular awareness (your focus), you'll have while being within the experience itself. In other words, you decide what your focal point is, and then let the whole of reality come to you equally.

Think of it in much the same way as your peripheral vision works. Even when you focus on something, like your phone, there's still your peripheral vision capturing the entire area around it. Mindfulness feels similar to when you look at an object, and then shift your focus to your peripheral vision. Your focus is on a single object, but you experience everything that comes into your field of awareness. There is no dividing reality in mindfulness, you take it all in as one body.

This is distinctly different from consciousness, which works more like a scanner scanning its environment for changes and obstructions. Consciousness is not all-inclusive, it only *scans* the totality of the present reality. The key is in what it misses, and this is why mindfulness is powerful. Mindfulness, a greater level of awareness, is our gateway to the true nature of reality. It captures reality "as it is" in its wholeness.

Why is this important? It's because we're always observing a fragmented or skewed version of reality that we amass so much stress and anxiety. Mindfulness completes the picture for us, first with regards to our awareness, bringing new things to light, and therein secondly with regards to a deeper understanding of life.

With your natural state of consciousness, you're constantly scanning for and trying to navigate what you believe are obstacles and problems. All you're ever trying to do is *move, get ahead,* or *do the next thing.* Mindfulness isn't a scattered awareness like consciousness, it's a complete form of awareness, the silent observing of the fantastic nature of things as one whole body, not as some separate thing which you must navigate and defend yourself from. This is a major reason why mindfulness leads to greater peace and tranquility, it's in those moments of mindfulness that you're living *as you were intended to live.* Or in other words, those things which block your perception vanish and you realize you're one with the whole vibration of life. Mindfulness shows us that we don't need to keep moving, going forward, pushing on, that we don't need to get that "thing" to find peace, and that we don't need to change *anything*, but rather that peace exists right here and right now.

A Note on Language:

The act of being mindful, of being fully awake to the present moment, can never be fully expressed in words.

Even the phrase "the present moment", although highly useful in getting you to visualize the correct process of being awake to reality, doesn't accurately explain mindfulness. For that reason, the present reality or just "reality" is a more accurate term, although it doesn't help visualize the process of being mindful as well as the "present moment" does, so throughout the book I'll be alternating between those and other various explanations to keep an accurate perspective.

Most importantly, know that mindfulness is to be personally experienced and practiced in your own life before you can fully grasp it. Never forget that language is a middle man, not the actual experience or thing itself which is being described. Grasping this point isn't just important when speaking of mindfulness, it's important with regards to *everything* in life.

Defining Mindfulness

Mindfulness isn't about quieting the mind, it's about observing the mind in its natural process silently without "you" ever stepping in.

The way we're used to living, the past and future are ever pressing up against us as if we were standing in between two moving walls that were slowly coming together. As we go about our lives we amass regret, and we torture ourselves over these regrets (often unconsciously). We wish we would have chosen one thing over another, we wish we wouldn't have said that, or we wish we would have made better decisions in general during a certain period of our lives. The past weighs down on many of us like an anvil and it affects everything that we do.

And then the future has us worried and attempting to control that which can't be controlled. We worry about everything, and the worst part is we balloon these worries to twice or three times their size and make them causes for stress and anxiety, even though what actually ends

up happening isn't usually nearly as bad as we imagined it would be.

And in an effort to control the outcome of our lives, the future keeps us constantly attempting to predict what's to come. We live in a perpetual state of prediction, often making the kinds of predictions that we don't even identify as predictions at all. We expect to be living in the same place for the next so many years, we expect (or plan to) be working at the same company for the next X years, we expect to be alive for another X years, or we expect to have our loved ones with us for so many more years.

But various microscopic predictions are made as well in our everyday lives: as we scan our environment with our surface-level consciousness we make judgments about the information that we take in. And based on that information, we take action. We do it all to make sure that nothing stands in the way of us accomplishing our task. That's what it's all about- consciousness, that is- it's a tool for scanning our environment for threats. We're constantly trying to control *everything*, never being willing to let go. This is how we operate, and so this is how we consequently live our entire lives.

We rarely, if ever, just sit back and observe reality as it is in the present moment. But if we can learn how to do this, if we can learn how to let go of the past and the future, imagination and all attachments, and exist fully in the present moment with mindfulness, we can tap into the ultimate tool for releasing ourselves from wrong perceptions, negative self-talk, limiting beliefs, attachments, and the need to control our lives and ultimately be able to discover true peace and happiness.

So then what actually *is* this mindfulness we keep talking about? Mindfulness is difficult to explain in a single sentence. It's an experience, and any attempt language makes to describe it always falls short, which is why it has been defined in many different ways and by many different people. Mindfulness is *a complete awareness of the present reality*. That's the most accurate definition I can give you. The only problem? It doesn't give you a very clear picture of what the process of actually *being mindful* is like, and this is arguably more important than attempting an accurate definition of mindfulness for the sake of knowledge.

The word awareness doesn't quite help you visualize the process of being mindful very well. At least to me it doesn't. Mindfulness is a conscious effort, not something that happens by itself, which is what awareness gives the impression of. It's not a hard concentration though, it's a subtle process of simply getting out of your mind and deciding that you're completely present to your life in this

Buddhaimonia
ZEN FOR EVERYDAY LIFE

moment (and every moment thereafter). To become mindful of something feels as if you said to yourself, "I'm awake", and instantaneously went from being completely asleep to wide awake. It's like the feeling you get when you open your eyes as wide as you possibly can, but more subtle. This feeling starts off especially subtle in the beginning, and strengthens as you practice. And mindful awareness is *always* centered on an object in the present moment (generally an object *in action*, not stationary). The act of focusing on an object in the present moment is generally called one's concentration, and the greater awareness you employ once "locking in" to said object is your mindfulness. Again, it's a subtle concentration, not a head-splitting level of attention on an object. You're not trying to push everything away, ***you're simply anchoring yourself in the present moment by keeping your focus on a central point.***

So then, what's a good visual definition of mindfulness, one which allows us to visualize the process of actually being mindful and can help us learn how to practice it? Using what we just discussed, the "visual" definition of mindfulness could be:

The process of simply paying attention in a specific, subtle, and yet wakeful manner to the present moment evenly (in its entirety), usually while attempting to keep a central point of attention on an object in that moment.

This definition helps us visualize the process of actually being mindful, and therefore is the definition you should use as a starting point when developing your practice.

A note on the nonjudgmental aspect of mindfulness: mindfulness is in fact a nonjudgmental awareness, and remembering this can help you practice, but I feel it's easier to remember that mindfulness is "the process of simply paying attention", and nothing more, therefore you shouldn't be purposely thinking anything. Another point is that no matter how hard you try thoughts will rise to the surface about what you're observing. Therefore to say that mindfulness itself is nonjudgmental is correct, but to say that you'll be nonjudgmental while being mindful is another thing entirely! But this is perfectly normal, and in no way a bad thing. You want to notice when you have these various thoughts and feelings. Mindfulness isn't about quieting the mind, it's about observing the mind in its natural process silently without "you" ever stepping in.

Being Mindful and the 3 Levels of Awareness

Let's take this a step further. What, then, does mindfulness look like when applying it to your everyday life? It doesn't always look the same. The version of mindfulness, or greater awareness, which has become so popular in the West is the most "concentrated" version. We'll call it level 1. In this "level of awareness" or level of mindfulness as we'll call them, you focus completely on an object-at least as much as your subtle concentration will allow, which will create more of a 70/30 or 80/20 split in attention for your object of meditation and everything else in your field of awareness respectively- such as your breath during sitting meditation, or your steps during walking meditation. You direct a subtle concentration to your object of meditation, ideally in a place of peace and quiet so that there's little to no distractions, and simply let your mindfulness do its thing. Acting as the "silent observer" of reality, your mindfulness catches everything that steps into your field of awareness. If you're sitting in meditation, focusing on your in breath and out breath, and a thought, feeling, or sensation arises, your mindfulness simply catches that thought, feeling, or sensation and gently acknowledges it nonjudgmentally.

This is why mindfulness is the silent observer. It simply observes everything in reality within what your field of awareness can view and never steps in to judge the situation. And once you've gently acknowledged the distraction, you simply come back to your breath. Imagine you were having a conversation with someone, and out of nowhere another person walked up and began talking to you. They just completely jumped into the conversation you were having and began talking over the other person. Now imagine trying to continue focusing your conversation on the other person. You couldn't. This stranger, who is literally speaking over them, would be too distracting. This gentle acknowledgment you make and the proceeding refocusing on your object of meditation during mindfulness is like turning to look at and speak directly with the person who walked up and stepped in the middle of your conversation, shaking their hand, and kindly letting them know that you can't talk because you were already in the middle of a conversation. Then, finally, turning away from the person to refocus on your original conversation. It's important not to treat these arising thoughts, feelings, and sensations as interruptions. They aren't bad, in fact it's good to notice these things arise while sitting in

Buddhaimonia
ZEN FOR EVERYDAY LIFE

meditation, it means you've developed your awareness enough to see them clearly. This is a very good thing and shows that your practice is developing.

This first level of awareness is the most focused, it deals with the fewest amount of outside distractions, but is more concentrated than the other two levels of awareness which occur in more of an everyday life situation. In most cases, the first level of awareness is reserved for sitting meditation, but if you have peace and quiet you can practice walking meditation, sweeping, washing the dishes, and other various activities in much the same way.

In this first level of awareness, you can often feel as though you've dissolved into the object of meditation itself. In sitting meditation for instance, your focused attention on your breath can sometimes give rise to the feeling that you've become one with your breath, as if the rest of you no longer existed. This "dropping away of mind and body" is a very deep and enriching experience, as if you died and were reborn with each in breath and out breath. In this moment, you can sense subtly a vast wisdom that stretches beyond space and time. Don't attempt to discern this state of selflessness, just be completely attentive of the experience, and let your intuition guide you.

Of course, being in such a state of heightened attention is nice, but our lives only offer us a small percentage of peace and quiet, which is why it's highly useful to be aware of the other two levels of awareness.

When we drive our car, walk down the street or through the office, eat with friends and family, or sit in any public location, we're in a much busier setting than when sitting in the quiet solitude of our home. These situations call for the second level of awareness. The second level of awareness is a much broader form of awareness. If you're driving your car to or from work, it's more than just focusing on your hands holding and moving the wheel and being mindful of the occasional thought, feeling, or sensation. This level of awareness understands that there are multiple important points of attention, such as your feet on the pedals, the traffic signs, and other cars. So imagine this level of awareness working more like a headlamp, viewing everything in your field of awareness as mindfulness always does, but with multiple points of focus.

This level of awareness is such a valuable tool in our everyday lives. Once you begin practicing, you'll see that to practice the first level of awareness while going about your everyday life is very difficult, therefore the opportunities are few. This level of awareness, on the other hand, is

Buddhaimonia
ZEN FOR EVERYDAY LIFE

built for it. The second level of mindfulness watches the hustle and bustle, it sees the many things which occur in your everyday life, and can accept them all openly without being overwhelmed. It sees when you become frustrated, when you get angry, when you slow down or speed up, and when you become tired. It notices the many things which pull you away from reality- the many advertisements, the people walking on the street, the gossip in the office, and the distractions on your phone. All three levels of mindfulness, or wise attention, are important in their own right, but if you have any semblance of a "normal" or modern life then you'll use the second level of awareness more than any other.

Throughout the remainder of the book I provide instruction on dozens of various exercises, many of which use mindfulness. While reading these various instructions keep in mind that you could apply either the first or second level of awareness depending on where you are when you're practicing. Sitting in meditation, for instance, is generally done with the first level, unless you find yourself sitting in a waiting room waiting to be called and decide to practice following your breath, in which case the second level of awareness may be better if there's constant distractions going on in the room such as a running T.V. or other people in conversation. Driving is the opposite instance. Driving is almost always done with the second level of awareness, unless you're driving alone down an empty road, but even then being in level one awareness is only temporary until you get to a stop sign or street light, otherwise it's dangerous. Lastly, there are some practices which are split down the middle. When eating, cleaning, or walking, you may have peace and quiet or you may be with or around other people. In such cases, you'll have to judge when to use which level of awareness.

A good point of reference is to attempt to use the highest level of awareness, level 1, and see if you feel any tension or difficulty due to too many outside distractions, particularly when you have to jump between more than one point of attention (like the driving example). If this is the case, relax your attention a bit to those multiple points of importance and let your awareness move more freely between them.

But there is one last, third, level of awareness which I haven't yet mentioned. This level of awareness expands your attention like a blanket covering a field. It simply observes the present reality completely with no particular point of focus. Imagine literally just being mindful of the present reality in and of itself. The whole picture, all at once, is your point of focus. Just as, when focusing your vision on an object, you make the decision to expand your vision peripherally and can then see everything within your field of vision equally, so are you mindful of everything within your field of awareness all at once.

This level of awareness is used for the highest level of distraction. It can be used either in a place of incredible distraction, where noises or other distractions are so pervading that it's nearly impossible to stay focused on any number of points of attention in any moment, or during a moment of incredible stress or anxiety, where your ability to focus has all but jumped out of the window and to even attempt to concentrate feels uncomfortable. It's the softest and subtlest of all the levels of awareness, like a gentle light that pervades everything. In that moment, you can often sense yourself *in* other things, as if you had expanded out indefinitely. Only you know it's not "you" in the sense of a separate self, because much the same way as when you sit in meditation and lose yourself in your breath, your sense of self dissolves in the experience.

This third level of awareness is to be used when you just can't stay in the second level of awareness no matter how hard you try. You have no ability to focus any sliver of your attention on anything and need to expand or "relax" your awareness in a sense. It can, though, also be used for the sake of itself. It's a nice practice to do from time to time, especially when you're in nature. To sit down and simply experience the totality of the present reality is a beautiful and nourishing practice which I suggest everyone learn how to do.

An easy example of this practice is to single out a sensory experience, like sound or sight, and simply sit while letting your awareness expand to all sounds or sights within your field of awareness. If you're sitting on your porch, on a park bench, or somewhere else similar while directing your awareness to the many sounds around you then pay attention to the sounds of the passing cars, the whistling trees, the chirping birds, the howling of the wind, and anything else that arises. You can even use this as a pre or post meditation practice by letting yourself rest in this state of complete awareness for a few minutes before starting your meditation session in order to help yourself relax.

I didn't mention this third level of awareness earlier with regards to the exercises throughout the book that include mindfulness because it, for the most part, is its own separate exercise. Keep this third level of mindfulness in mind when in a situation that doesn't allow you to focus on any object of meditation as well as an additional and very beneficial practice in itself to add into your everyday life.

There is no best form of awareness. They each have their place, and learning how and when

to use them is key in getting the most from your practice. For the most part, you'll be able to decipher the best situations for each form of awareness from your personal experience. Use all 3 to shine the light of mindfulness on your entire life, as opposed to just spending 10 minutes a day sitting in meditation. The more often you practice, the more beneficial your practice will be.

Discovering Freedom in Everyday Life

Make the choice to live freely in your everyday life, awake to the peace that exists in each moment.

What is your everyday life? Really, what is it? What does it all mean when you're cooking dinner, driving to work, walking to the store, or working on that big project? When you're walking down the street, is it a serious affair? Or is it, and the rest of your life, a playful adventure? Just one big playful adventure, waiting for you to bust out and become alive to the freedom that's always existed within and around you.

Most people have the wrong idea about freedom. Sure, there's certain basic freedoms that are important, and we definitely weren't meant to

sit behind desks for eight hours each day, but most of us have the wrong perception that freedom exists only in the tangible things we can touch and feel. This concept of what true freedom actually is couldn't be more wrong. True freedom exists not outside, but *inside*.

When you walk, do you walk with your worries and challenges hanging heavy over your shoulders, obsessing over your next "big move", or do you walk fully aware of the absolute freedom that exists in each moment? If you know how to walk fully present for each new moment, aware of the true nature of reality, you'll see that you're already free in the widest sense. Whether you have enough money to pay your bills, are at a job that you hate, or are having trouble in your relationship, you can tap into the true freedom that is this moment. This freedom is vital because it's altogether necessary for you to experience complete peace of mind. Without it, peace of mind will stay a far-off image, always just far enough away that you can't reach it.

When we're fully awake to the present moment, all boundaries disappear and we realize our true nature. And our true nature is that of absolute freedom. Every day, every hour, and every moment you have a choice. You have the choice to awaken to the present reality and the peace of your true nature, or to continue living only semi-

conscious to the world around you. Make the choice to live freely in your everyday life, awake to the peace that exists in each moment.

Living Deeply

...to live your life deeply, aware of your interbeing, cultivates in you a deep reverence for life and an unshakeable sense of gratitude that pervades everything that you do.

In a given day, how many different "things" do you think you pass by? I mean everything-street signs, the pavement in the street, your car and the many things within it, the various items in your kitchen, bedroom, bathroom, as well as the trees, grass, bushes and flowers outside. Have you ever taken a second just to think about any of these "things"?

What I mean is, have you ever taken a second to think *really* deeply about any of these things? Matter of fact, anything in your life? Maybe you have, but weren't exactly sure what to think about what you had found. Maybe you did and felt you had a special experience that you just couldn't put your finger on. My guess is probably not, as we don't usually think all that deeply about anything in our everyday lives.

I don't mean look at a glass of orange juice and stare at it closely, looking at all the tiny pieces of pulp floating around and how they get carried around as the juice swishes back and forth in your cup. I mean thinking about the *nature* of the juice. Have you ever thought about what the true nature of the orange juice really is? If we were to do this, where would we start?

Well, it would start with where you got the orange juice- the store. And where did the store get it? Possibly nearby, although likely thousands of miles away from your location, transported generally via a series of 18-wheeler trucks. Where did the trucks get it from? At a facility where dozens of workers and machines labored to extract the group of oranges that would eventually make up your juice into the juice itself, concentrated it, and ultimately packaged it into its nice neat little container. Before that, it was an orange picked from a farm, where farmers added various chemicals and sweeteners, fortified the orange with additional vitamins, and worked carefully to maintain the ideal environment for the orange to grow. Before it was an orange ready to be picked, it was a newly sprouted bud being fed nutrients from the orange tree, which absorbed its nutrients from the soil around where its roots rested. So then, where did the orange bud come from? Before then, did it not exist? Well, you could say the "potential" for the orange always existed within the tree's DNA, so then, what was the orange tree before it was an orange tree? A seed? What helped the seed grow? The very same soil. And what was in the soil? A whole lot of different things. And where did the seed come from originally? We could do this all day, but you get the point.

Now let's come back to the orange juice for a second. Look at it, *really* look at it. That's the real orange juice. The orange juice which, when looked at deeply enough, we see could never have existed if it weren't for each and every element that contributed to its growth and eventual "maturation". The juicing facility? The farm and its farmers? The orange tree? The nutrients from the soil? The soil itself? The orange juice coming to be, sitting in front of you as it were, depended on each and every one of these things. If you were to take away even one of these elements, the orange juice would never have existed.

Now consider this: everything in life is just like this. Try it for yourself some time. Pick an object- any object- and follow it as far back as you can. If you don't know how it got to you, look it up online or go to your local library and search for a book on the subject. Sit back and think about that for a moment. *Every single thing around you is*

Buddhaimonia
ZEN FOR EVERYDAY LIFE

just like the orange juice. And I don't just mean your coffee cup, your coffee, your computer, your desk, your chair, your couch, etc. I also mean *you.* Specifically, I mean that if you were to think deeply enough about yourself, about your life, you'd see that you yourself depend on so many different things just to exist right here in this moment (and other things depend on you).

You depend on the many farmers of the world to provide you the crops that eventually end up on your dinner plate, you depend on the vast systems of filtering and plumbing to deliver the water you depend on to survive every day, and if people didn't buy the product or service that you, your company, or the company you work for sell, your livelihood would be wiped out. Let's not forget about the thousands of hospitals and medical centers, doctors, nurses, and medical supplies we all at one point or another depend on to help us recover from illness or injury. And if your body didn't do its job, the job it does so well automatically without you ever even having to think about it, you'd be dead and gone or sitting like a vegetable on a hospital bed. And that's just a few examples of the many things we depend upon.

You being here as you are also depends on numerous things *not* happening on a daily basis that happen to thousands of other people every single day. You just being alive depends on: you not getting into a car accident, you not being run over by a car, the plane you were just on not crashing, your body not shutting down, no one harming you, you not contracting a virus, you not contracting a disease, and so on.

And your lifestyle? It depends on literally millions of different things. Have a computer? Internet? A smartphone? Phone service? A T.V.? Cable? Ever go out to eat? Fast food? The food in your fridge? Shop at a mall? Or a department store? Your insurance? Savings? I could literally go on forever. Without the millions of people involved in bringing all of those things to you and the countless materials harnessed from nature required to craft them, your life would be unrecognizable.

What about your parents? Think about all the work they did to raise you, and all the things that had to align the way that they did throughout your life for you to be sitting here now reading this book. What if your parents had never met? What if that person that changed your life had decided never to help you? What if you had never gotten that lucky break?

Let's go back to the orange juice for a second. When you drink the orange juice, what happens? Does it disappear forever? No, it merely takes another form. The orange juice goes through your body, distributing the various vitamins, minerals,

and chemicals which were once a part of the orange juice to different parts of your body, and then the waste is removed. Where does the orange juice go? Like water turning to ice or ice turning to water, everything in life is constantly changing form. Never disappearing, we're all walking together in an infinite dance of interconnected interdependence.

What's the point of all this? To show you that the natural state of life is both an interconnectedness and interdependence between all things, including yourself. When you wake up in the morning, what's your first thought? Do you immediately start worrying about how you're going to finish that project by the deadline, how you're going to make ends meet this month, whether that person likes you or not, or do you remind yourself of how fortunate you are to have another 24 beautiful hours to live?

If you can learn to live in a way that you're constantly aware of your interbeing, a term referring to the way that everything in life is constantly at play with one another both interconnected and interdependent on one another, you can live each moment of your life with reverence and gratitude. Each moment of life becomes beautiful, fascinating, and full of peace. Not a single moment of life is wasted because not a single minute moment of life is without

Buddhaimonia
ZEN FOR EVERYDAY LIFE

significance. It *all* has meaning. Each and every single little moment of life has the most significant meaning that it's almost too deep for us to fathom. To live in this way is to have such a deep reverence for life that you can't help but feel grateful to be alive and at peace with the world around you.

If you look deep enough, if you take something and follow it as far as it will go, it always dissolves into the ultimate. That is, it always dissolves into nothingness. But this nothingness isn't a blank and empty nothingness, it's a place where all things "come to be". It's where the great potential of life exists all at once, and all of life blossoms from it. If anything in life is the "spiritual" level, this is it. It's a place where you recognize that it's more than just us being interconnected and interdependent, but that each and every one of us is a dewdrop reflecting the entire cosmos from within ourselves. To go much further is beyond the scope of *Zen for Everyday Life*, but just know that to live your life deeply, aware of your interbeing, cultivates in you a deep reverence for life and an unshakeable sense of gratitude that pervades *everything* that you do. Living in such a way brings a profound sense of peace and joy to your life as a whole.

Contemplation and Mindfulness

Buddhaimonia
ZEN FOR EVERYDAY LIFE

Contemplation is the act of looking deeply, or closely examining, a thing so as to see into the true nature of it, and it's the second tool in the *Zen for Everyday Life* arsenal. In some ways, contemplation can seem very similar to mindfulness. Ultimately, mindfulness could easily be looked at as the act of looking deeply at something, although that's mostly a byproduct. The purpose of mindfulness is to rest in an open, spacious, and nonjudgmental state of mind so as to observe reality in its true state. Contemplation often then takes over where mindfulness leaves off. Contemplation and mindfulness are constantly at play with one another, so much so to where it's often impossible to tell them apart. The easiest way to look at it is they're both ultimately forms of meditation, and leave it at that (although there is both an active and passive form of contemplation, which need to be differentiated).

While mindful, in an open state of awareness, various things will rise to the surface of your consciousness. Once this happens, contemplation takes over and allows you to look deeply into the nature of that which arose. Let's take anger for instance. You've been meditating for a few months now and this uncomfortable feeling of anger seems to keep arising within you. You're not sure where it's coming from, but you continue to acknowledge it nonjudgmentally so that it can further rise to the surface of your consciousness.

At this point, you can "sit with" your anger. That is, you can sit in a meditative contemplation, allowing your mind to gently focus its attention on the anger. Follow the anger as far as it will let you go. To sit with an emotion, with a feeling, in this way is like sitting in a sauna and allowing yourself to "sweat out" the so-called impurities in your body. This is an example of a passive form of contemplation, using your subtle intuition to guide yourself, and is very similar to sitting in meditation. On the contrary, a more active form of contemplation is like what we did with the orange, where we journeyed through the history of the orange to realize its interbeing with all those elements it came in contact with, including ourselves.

Transforming Pain and Suffering

...by diminishing the ego's power we can transform our lives from one of constant pain and a sense of something always being missing, to a life filled with peace where we know that we're absolutely and completely whole.

Buddhaimonia
ZEN FOR EVERYDAY LIFE

In "Letting Go", we covered 11 major misconceptions with regards to finding peace and happiness in everyday life. Once you remove these various illusions and rid yourself of false notions that something you should have done in the past or something you need in the future will make you happy or bring you peace, what's left? All that's left is *now*. The present moment. This can be beautiful, but it can also be uncomfortable too. By seeing deeply into the truth of our lives and realizing that acquiring something isn't going to solve our problems, that we're altogether complete and not lacking in any way and can find peace right now if we're willing to do what it takes, we both realize the beauty of the present moment and are forced to face our problems all at the same time.

But the *only* way that you'll find peace and happiness is by facing your pain and suffering. If you think that you can run from your problems and at the same time find peace and happiness then you'll never get where you're trying to go.

Everything exists all at once in the present moment: our pain and suffering as well as our peace and happiness. We live reminiscing over and regretting the past as well as looking forward to and fantasizing about the future because the present moment holds too much pain. But this is also where our peace of mind exists.

Buddhaimonia
ZEN FOR EVERYDAY LIFE

When we live in the present moment, everything drops away. This is because, in reality, there *is* no yesterday and no tomorrow, only the peace of the present moment truly exists. This is reality. If you rest long enough in the present moment all of your stresses and difficulties will rise to the surface like the carbonation in a soda. And, just like the carbonation in a soda, if you rest long enough in the present moment the path to freedom will present itself. Your stresses, negative self-talk, and limiting beliefs will dissolve and become transformed.

We all have different things we need to overcome, but for most of us, it's some form of negative self-talk which plagues our thinking and inhibits our actions. Mindfulness, just as in the carbonation example, helps these messages we repeatedly loop in our heads rise to the surface so that we can identify and confront them. Once they've risen to the surface, we merely have to realize that they're not a part of us, that they're completely separate and something we choose to hold onto or not. That's when you can choose to let go and separate yourself from it.

Many of us struggle for years, if not our entire lives, trying to "find ourselves". But what does this really mean? A more accurate explanation of this would be that we're trying to find a place for ourselves. That we're trying to

define ourselves. But this is the work of none other than the ego. The ego is the force which is constantly at work attempting to make you think that you're this separate self apart from everyone and everything else. It's not some real aspect of yourself though, it's a complete illusion. By diminishing the ego's power we can transform our lives from one of constant pain and a sense of *something* always being missing, to a life filled with peace where we know that we're absolutely and completely whole.

This is the most important point of all. We all think we're missing something. But what is it that we're missing? Some of us think we know, some of us don't. Some of us get it, and realize that what we thought it is isn't it, and some of us never get that thing, or never find out what it is. But this is all one great big lie, the most damaging of all lies. You're not missing anything. You're complete just as you are. You're not missing a screw, you're not lacking something, you don't need your true love to complete yourself, and you're not messed up. You're absolutely perfect *just as you are*.

My whole life I was always searching for that *something* to complete me. For me, it came in the form of my self-worth and what I'd accomplished with my life (or rather, had not accomplished). I always felt this sense of incompleteness because I hadn't accomplished anything of value. I always felt like a screw up and a nobody because I didn't have a nice car, custom suits, and a big house.

When I began practicing mindfulness, and really seeking to live my life with greater awareness, or "wise" attention, I finally felt like I had woken up. In those moments of being mindful, I felt as if I had awoken from a long slumber and discovered an amazing new world. With mindfulness you tap into the peace that is everything you do. Every step, every breath, every conversation, and everything you drink and eat. Everything becomes a chance to renew your sense of inner peace and happiness because everything is this altogether whole and vibrant experience.

But it wasn't always beautiful, sometimes it felt uncomfortable, and at first I couldn't figure out why. But I quickly began to notice that what was happening was certain things were rising to the surface of my consciousness, and these things weren't always positive. Little did I know, but I began the process of unravelling myself. Much in the way that the sun rises slowly in the morning over the skyline, as I practiced more and more my eyes gradually awakened to the whole of my being. I saw things I didn't like, things that I didn't know were there. But I also began seeing that these things weren't in fact me at all, and rather separate from me. Once I had gotten to that point, the point where these things which laid hidden in my consciousness had risen to the surface and became perfectly visible, I was able to transform them by seeing that they weren't me at all. At that point, I simply chose to let go of them. That is, to stop believing those things about myself. And just like that, they were gone.

Like reading a good book, the path to discovering your true self is fascinating and exciting, so much so to where once you begin you'll find it difficult to stop. It won't always be easy, but it will be beautiful, and ultimately lead to a sense of peace you've never felt before.

Mindfulness, living deeply with contemplation, and overall adopting a daily practice of peace doesn't just help us overcome our negative self-talk and limiting beliefs though. There's more to the pain and suffering that exists in life than just your own personal issues of course. That is, most of us have pain in the form of the loss of a loved one, depression, a rough break up or divorce, or something else. And there's no getting around these things. No matter how much money you gain, no matter how much power you amass, and no matter how wise you become, you'll still have adversity. This is just a part of life. But what's important isn't whether or not we can get rid of these things, it's how we react to and look at them. Learn how to nourish your mind and body and

Buddhaimonia
ZEN FOR EVERYDAY LIFE

you'll be able to transform your pain and suffering into peace and happiness.

Finding Meaning

When we lack a sense of meaning or purpose in life, it's because we're distanced from reality and the world around us. Imagine you were walking on a surface with low gravity. Far from being grounded, you'd float away aimlessly without anything you could do about it. You'd think you needed external forces to help keep you rooted to the ground, and constantly be in search of *something* to help you accomplish that. But that something never existed, so there was never anything for you to find.

When we learn how to live in the present moment and become deeply in touch with reality, we become grounded and can weather any storm that comes our way. Our center becomes deeply rooted to the source of things and every step, every turn, every action, and every thought becomes an act of the entire cosmos.

If we want to discover a sense of meaning in our life, we need to learn how to live deeply. We need to live in a way that we're constantly aware of our interbeing with all human and non-human things. By doing this, you'll see that every

seemingly small action carries with it a great significance, and you'll never search for a sense of meaning in your life again.

*Look at it, **really** look at it.*

Zen for Everyday Life covers numerous ways you can use contemplation, whether passive or active, in your daily life. But above what's mentioned in the proceeding chapters, remember that you can use contemplation in each and every moment of your day. Pick an object, even yourself, and take it as far as it will let you go. Really look into the true nature of the thing you're contemplating. Feeling uncomfortable today, but can't figure out why? Sit for a while, passively being aware of this uncomforting feeling, and see what arises. You could even take something outside of yourself that you don't like and use active contemplation to pursue it to its end, seeing that it's not what you originally thought it was. You could even do this with people, helping cultivate compassion and understanding for them.

Buddhaimonia
ZEN FOR EVERYDAY LIFE

Part II: Being Peace

Sitting

If you want to discover the true meaning of Zen in your everyday life, you have to understand the meaning of keeping your mind on your breathing and your body in the right posture in zazen.

- Shunryu Suzuki, *Zen Mind, Beginner's Mind*

In Zen, the practice of sitting meditation is called "zazen", which translates directly to sitting, or seated, meditation in Japanese. Modern day Zen schools are split into two major sects: Soto and Rinzai. Zazen is the cornerstone of Soto Zen practice, the larger of the two traditional Zen sects (but plays a part in all of Zen).

In the Soto lineage of Zen, practitioners will sometimes sit and meditate for what can seem like inhuman lengths of time, as much as 18 hours in a day for multiple days in a row. It's difficult to imagine a higher level of discipline than the level that these Zen students place on their practice. Giving up normal life to be a monk or nun can already be difficult enough for some, but a

Buddhaimonia
ZEN FOR EVERYDAY LIFE

schedule which, as much as one week every month for some monasteries, requires students to meditate for ¾ of every waking hour in a given week, is the ultimate level of dedication.

Of course, they don't always meditate for these lengths of time. On an average day, they might meditate for one 30 minute to 1 ½ hour period shortly upon waking, then again some 3-4 times before the day is over, totaling somewhere between 4-8 hours of zazen with short periods of walking meditation (or "kinhin" in Japanese) after most zazen sessions as well as 3 meals, drinking tea, cleaning, sometimes reading depending on the teacher, and a little bit of break time in between. And *everything* is done in mindfulness.

This is the level of importance they place on the practice of zazen. For these Soto Zen practitioners, "satori", or a sudden awakening, is the chief aim of their practice. But in Zen, as opposed to other spiritual traditions, practitioners simply sit in zazen to express their true nature. You don't sit in meditation to achieve some amazing stage of greater awakening, you're already perfectly enlightened right here in this moment.

If that didn't seem to make sense, good! It means you're paying attention. To live Zen is to live in a way that you express your true nature, which means, in a way, to exist "naturally" without attempting to direct your life in any way. Or in other words, realizing yourself as a living expression of the universe and ceasing any "pushing or pulling" against the natural flow of things. This is how Soto Zen students seek to live. This is why, while the intention is to achieve satori, Zen students live in a way that they don't strive for it (or anything else) as someone would strive towards a goal, fighting their way through life and therefore causing friction with the natural flow of things.

This is a point which can't be fully put into words, but it's best you don't think too hard on it anyway. You should simply sit in zazen with no intention, no goal, and no expectations whatsoever. Just sit, and you'll naturally express your boundless nature. Your job is simply to sit long enough that you can tune into this wondrous vibration.

Zazen

In order to begin feeling the benefits of a daily zazen practice, all you need to do is begin sitting. That's the most important thing to do right now. Simply start sitting. Five minutes, ten minutes, one hour, it doesn't matter. Simply work on sitting every day, even if just once a day, and make it a daily practice. I'd suggest meditating early in the morning, but only after you've drunk your morning coffee or tea. Don't just get up and start meditating as it's very difficult, and largely useless, to try meditating while half-asleep as you'll just be falling asleep constantly.

Zazen is relatively simple. There's just a few important points you need to follow:

Sit

✿ *Find the right sitting position for you.* Preferably, in a quiet place with little to no possible interruptions. Here are the most common:

a. *Lotus.* Ideally, you want to strive to sit in the lotus position. Making your body into a tripod, the lotus position is the most stable sitting position available to us. To sit in the lotus position, start off in a typical cross-legged position. Now, take your left leg and place it on the top of your right thigh (as high up on your thigh as you can place it). Next, take your right leg and place it on top of your left thigh. Lastly, slide your bottom back ever so slightly in a quick motion to strengthen your posture. The lotus position can be really uncomfortable in the beginning. But keep at it, it's definitely

worth it. Eventually the pain will subside and you'll be able to sit without feeling much of anything.

b. *Half-lotus.* As I mentioned, in the beginning the lotus position can be really difficult to sit in. If you can manage it though, I'd suggest sitting through the pain of the full lotus and getting used to it, as it will be a great help to your practice. If that's not possible though, start with the half lotus. The half lotus is simply half of the lotus position: just place your left leg over your right thigh (or right leg over your left thigh). If you sit regularly in the half lotus, you should alternate regularly with the right leg on the left thigh as this will help get both legs used to the positioning. Then, with practice, you'll begin to be able to sit in the full lotus.

c. *Chair.* If the half lotus isn't possible then it's perfectly acceptable to simply sit in a chair. Place your feet flat on the ground and put a pillow between your lower back and the back of the chair to keep your back straight. No matter how you sit, it's important to use a pillow or a zafu (a Zen meditation pillow). A cushion isn't necessary, but it definitely helps. A zafu/pillow greatly improves stability, strengthens your posture, and makes sitting more comfortable. For the full or half lotus positions, sit on the last third or so of the pillow (you can fold a typical bed pillow in half and sit on that). If you're sitting in the lotus position this will bring your other knee down to the floor, creating a very stable tripod. If you don't use a pillow one knee will stick up slightly while you're in the lotus position, leading to less stability and comfort.

🌀 *Posture.* First, take a few deep breaths. Stretch your back, neck, shoulders, and arms a bit and relax the muscles in your face by forming a half-smile. Also, make sure to relax your abdomen. Both the face and abdomen are places we're so used to tensing that we don't even notice it. We build up a lot of tension in our bodies throughout each day, and it's important to take a second to release that tension in order to remove any possible discomfort and distraction during meditation. Now, let's form the proper posture. Improper posture can cause a whole host of trouble: back pain, obstructed breathing, and even serve as a distraction in itself. So first, your spine should be straight with the back of your neck pushed up slightly towards the sky. Next, tilt your chin down ever so slightly to strengthen your posture (an inch, at most). Lastly, rock back and forth in order to find the most stable resting position for your body so that you're not leaning during your meditation. Rocking helps you find the most stable sitting position and in doing so removes a potential distraction during meditation.

🌀 *Hands.* In Zen, Buddhism, and any of the other ancient Indian spiritual traditions such as Yoga, mudrās are used as hand placements meant to symbolize important principles and improve the flow of oxygen to the body during meditation. Mudrā is a Sanskrit word meaning "seal", "mark", or "gesture", and in Zen practitioners form the "cosmic" mudrā while meditating. The cosmic mudrā is meant to symbolize the highest awakening, or the interbeing of all things. In order to form the cosmic mudrā, place your hands in your lap with palms facing up. Place one hand on top of the other, the dominant hand's finger joints on top of the other hand's finger joints so that your dominant hand's fingers overlap the other hand's. Thumbs touching at the tips, forming an oval shape. The cosmic mudrā helps place your focus on the "hara", or spiritual center of the body, which is located 2 inches below your naval (breath is where mind and body merge, and your breath should come from deep within your abdomen at this point). Placing the hara as your point of attention brings mind, body and breath together as one and assists you in following your breath. Keep in mind, this step isn't necessary to sit and meditate, it's simply meant to enhance your practice.

🌀 *Eyes.* Look downwards some 3-4 feet in front of you and let your eyelids drop naturally, they'll fall about halfway shut, as intended. You want your eyes partially open to keep you fully aware and awake (eyes closed invites loss of concentration and dozing off), and by looking down you won't need to blink.

Breathe

🌀 *Be mindful.* Preferably, breathe in and out through your nose for deeper and more controlled breathing. If this isn't possible for you though then it's OK to breathe through your mouth. Be mindful of each in breath and out breath, it's your point of concentration during zazen. Observe your breath silently, don't attempt to control either your in breath or out breath. Your mindful breathing will calm your breathing naturally without any effort. Follow each complete in breath and out breath from start to finish. This will help you stay in mindfulness as well as make it easier to notice when you've lost your concentration and need to go back to your breath. The goal is to *make the effort* to be mindful of your breath as close to 100% of the time you're sitting as possible. Your effort won't be perfect, but that's not the point, just sit down with *the intention* to stay mindful of your breath 100% of the time. This shouldn't feel like you're forcefully trying to keep your awareness on your breath though, it should feel effortless and be gently aware of distractions in just the same manner.

⚘ *Count.* Count one at the end of the first inhale and two at the end of the first exhale. Continue like this until you get to 10, and then start the count over. You can call this "stage one". Every time a thought distracts you, simply start the 10 count over from 1. Do this until you can count to 10 with little to no effort. Then, count each inhale + exhale as one. And when that becomes easy, stop counting and simply follow your breath. We're naturally conditioned to want to rush through things, it feels good and we think that we've accomplished something, but it's important not to do this with meditation. However long it takes, make sure you don't cut corners and progress naturally. If you catch yourself being mindful of a thought that has arisen in your mind, don't keep counting- go back to your breath and start again from 1.

Be Mindful

✿ *Acknowledge.* It's perfectly natural for thoughts, feelings, and other sensations to come up when sitting in meditation. *Do not push them away* and don't label them as "bad". These thoughts and feelings are not bad or good, they're simply things which have arisen within your field of awareness and should be acknowledged. *Meditation is acceptance of everything, not avoidance.* When fear, anger, the source of our stress, the realization of wrong perceptions, and so many other things which rise to the surface during meditation arise in you is when you have the opportunity to become conscious of them and transform them for the better. In zazen, you're not trying to do anything, you're simply the silent observer of your own true nature. These various afflictions will run their course and dissipate on their own, your job is only to observe everything that steps inside your field of mindfulness. Each one of these afflictions, when transformed, will bring you greater peace of mind.

🌀 ***Be mindful (again).*** Let go of the thought, feeling, or sensation and return to your breath just as before. At first, you'll lose your focus constantly. Your mind will drift and bounce around endlessly, just know that it's a normal part of the process. Keep sitting and, with time, your mind will gain better and better clarity. And the more clarity you gain through your meditation the more at peace you'll be. Keep in mind though that the point isn't to have such a quiet mind that you never become distracted during meditation. Don't ever expect this to happen, nor do you need it to. The point is to quiet the mind *enough* to where you can sit and observe it clearly.

I'd suggest sitting in meditation once a day for simply five minutes at first. Let your body naturally tell you when it feels ready to move on to longer and longer periods of meditation. As you gain greater clarity and can sit with less of a monkey mind you'll naturally find yourself wanting to sit for longer periods. You can take your practice however far you'd like or keep it at five minutes, but as a general guidepost I'd suggest two daily sessions at about 30-45 minutes apiece.

It's impossible to describe what it feels like to sit in zazen as your mind begins to gain some decent level of clarity. It just feels right. Absolute peace is the only way I can describe it, and even that falls short of it. You'll just have to experience it for yourself.

Zen, On the Move

That might sound like a bit of a funny title, but one of the most important points to keep in mind about *Zen for Everyday Life* is the fact that it isn't a rigid book attempting to convince you that the only way to meditate is by sitting still in complete silence. Of course, there's nothing wrong with sitting meditation, but don't think the only way to greater peace of mind is to sit for long hours each day.

Did you know that at one point in China, during the "Golden Age of Zen" (Zen being "Cha'an" in Chinese) from about 400 to 1000 A.D., walking meditation was the primary practice? Centuries ago, monks would travel long distances, attempting to find a teacher who would give them that "spark" which would lead to their sudden

awakening. It was well understood that different teachers suited different students better, and so students would walk for miles traveling all around the country trying to find their ideal teacher.

Even when it comes to sitting meditation itself, you don't have to restrict yourself to sitting on a meditation cushion in a quiet room. What's the difference between sitting in your room in the morning and sitting in your office chair in the afternoon? Not all that much. Should you just forget your practice altogether when you're sitting at the office working for long hours? Not at all, anything can be done with greater awareness and there's a way to meditate in any situation.

When sitting at your desk, in a waiting room, or in a chair almost anywhere else you can always take a moment to follow your breath or become aware of the many sounds or sights within your field of awareness. Don't restrict your practice to the meditation cushion, get up and make your entire life into a living meditation.

Buddhaimonia
ZEN FOR EVERYDAY LIFE

Walking

To walk in this way is in fact to stop- to bring pause to the activity of the day and bring yourself back to the present moment.

When my youngest son Azriel was just a few months old, I'd often walk around with him secured to my chest with a baby carrier. It was comfortable for him, so much so that he'd often fall asleep in it, and so at night I'd sometimes quietly walk him around until he fell asleep.

While I did this, I'd practice walking meditation. I'd walk slowly and purposefully in either a large circle or pace back and forth until he fell asleep. It might sound funny, but this was my first experience with walking meditation. I meditated for nearly two years before trying walking meditation, and now it's a regular part of my practice (and possibly my "favorite" form of meditation).

I practice walking meditation any chance I get: when I walk to the restroom, when I walk down the hall to the kitchen, when I walk from my car to the store and vice versa, and especially whenever I leave home and walk to my car. This is my favorite time to practice walking meditation. In the morning, the sun is rising just above the skyline, there's a chill in the air, and the morning dew covers everything. And the afternoon and evening is just as beautiful to walk amongst. In California, where I've lived since I was just a few months old, the afternoon sky is almost always clear. I can see a few soft white clouds and blue sky as far as my eyes can reach. And in the evening I can see the many stars and almost feel my connection to them. I make sure not to take any of this for granted. Each time I walk to my car I do so slowly, appreciating the present moment.

In order to get from point A to point B, you need to walk. Even in the case of your car, the bus, or a plane, you need to walk to get there and walk to your destination once you get off. Everywhere you go is a chance to practice walking meditation. Sometimes you might be more compelled to walk fast, or at a medium pace. During walking meditation it's best to walk very slowly, but even at a medium pace, a pace more acceptable as you go about your day, it's a very nourishing and powerful practice.

If you're always on the move, and aren't used to getting (correction: taking) much time for yourself, walking meditation is a great practice to add on top of your once or twice daily practice of sitting meditation. You may have to practice sitting meditation for a few weeks before your mindfulness is strong enough to practice walking meditation properly, but it's worth it. Walking meditation has an incredible ability to put a stop to the constant rushing around that so many of us are used to. To walk in this way is in fact to stop- to bring pause to the activity of the day and bring yourself back to the present moment.

Even if you don't meditate every time you walk, and do so just once or twice a day, it can be a very beneficial practice. The combination of sitting and walking meditation already rounds out a daily practice of meditation nicely, as its one of the things we do most in a given day, which is why walking meditation is the second most common of all meditative practices. The steps to practicing walking meditation in some ways are identical to zazen, but with some changes, particularly the fact that you're following your steps as opposed to your breath:

Decide

Buddhaimonia
ZEN FOR EVERYDAY LIFE

🌀 ***Know where you're going.*** Before you begin, it's important to know where you're walking to. Make your destination a conscious decision- whether it's your car, home from your car, work from your car, the end of the street, your yard, or a tree. Know where you're going, set your mind to it, and then let go and forget about it altogether.

Walk

🌀 ***Match your steps with your breath.*** Do a little exercise: gauge how many naturally slow steps you take for each natural inhale as well as exhale. Don't attempt to control your breath, and try to just let your body naturally start walking on its own without your mind getting in the way. Likewise, just as when you're practicing sitting meditation, don't attempt to control your breath. Let each inhale and exhale flow out on its own without you interjecting.

🌀 ***Be mindful.*** Be mindful of each step you take. The process of being mindful of your steps can be broken down into three sections: *lifting (the foot), swinging (the foot forward), and placing (the foot down).* By focusing on this sequence, it will make it much easier to practice walking meditation. Be mindful of each complete step from start to finish. Complete one step with your right foot and then begin the next step, now being mindful of the next complete step with your left foot, and so on. Observe your steps silently, don't attempt to control your speed, just let yourself walk at a natural pace.

✿ *Count.* As opposed to counting as you did during sitting meditation, you can say "in" for each step on inhale and "out" for each step on exhale. So "in, in, in" on each inhale if you take 3 steps and "out, out, out" on each exhale for 3 more. It's important to count, say in/out, or something to that degree (to yourself) because you'll want a clear way to monitor when you've lost your concentration. If you prefer, you can repeat a phrase of some sort, particularly one that calms you. Just match the number of steps you're taking on each inhale or exhale with an equal number of syllables. So 3 steps on each inhale and then exhale could be "peace-is-now", five steps on each inhale and exhale could be "peace-is-this-mo-ment", and so on. You can make up whatever phrase you want, as long as the syllables match the number of steps.

Be Mindful

❧ *Acknowledge.* The instructions here are the same as in sitting meditation: It's perfectly natural for thoughts, feelings, and other sensations to come up when meditating. *Do not push them away* and don't label them as "bad". These thoughts and feelings are not bad or good, they're simply things which have arisen within your field of mindfulness and should be acknowledged. *Meditation is acceptance of everything, not avoidance.* When fear, anger, the source of our stress, the realization of wrong perceptions, and so many other things which rise to the surface during meditation arise in you is when you have the opportunity to become conscious of them and transform them for the better. In walking meditation ("kinhin" in Japanese, or as I like to call it "walking Zen"), you're not trying to do anything, you're simply being the silent observer of your own infinite nature. These various afflictions will run their course and dissipate on their own, your job is only to observe everything that steps inside your field of mindfulness. Each one of these afflictions, when transformed, will bring you greater peace of mind.

✿ *Be mindful (again).* Let go of the thought, feeling, or sensation and return to your steps just as before. When you walk, you may find yourself becoming distracted more often than when you sit in meditation. This is natural, as no matter where you walk there will be additional distractions. This is the reason you should practice sitting meditation for some time before beginning walking meditation. Once you build up your power of mindfulness, this won't be as much of a problem. If you still find yourself being distracted often though, remember the levels of awareness and simply slip from level 1 to level 2.

The Walk of Life

If you prefer to schedule a time to practice walking meditation, you can do that too. I'd suggest walking in nature, even if it's just walking barefoot on your front or backyard or at a park. Take your shoes off and walk barefoot on the grass. Take a second to feel the grass in between your toes, look up at the sky above, and feel the fresh air coming in and out of your lungs. Taking a second to relish in the moment is not only enjoyable but it helps you become more present before beginning your session of walking Zen. When you walk, walk very slowly. Find a natural pace, but remind yourself that you have nowhere to go- you're simply walking in order to walk and therefore should raise, swing, and place each foot down with great care as if it were the last thing you were to do.

It can be very nourishing to pause your meditation for a moment to imagine that you're simply a leaf from the great tree of life extending out of the earth. Imagine that each living being is a leaf on this tree, and just as the leaf of a tree is a part of the tree and yet at the same time may seem to have its own separate identity as a leaf, you may at times seem separate from the whole of life, but you're really a complete expression of the whole cosmos, interconnected to all other living and nonliving things.

Arriving

Each moment is unique, and the emotional energy we typically carry with us doesn't have to carry on from moment to moment.

We're constantly moving from one place to another: from work to our car, from our car to home, from home back to our car and off to work again, from home or work to running errands, visiting friends and family, and many other infinite variations and occasions. And we're always going from one situation to the another: from working on a project at the office to greeting our family at home, from fighting at home to presenting a new idea at the office, from being turned down to going back home to our family, and so on. Two problems arise out of this: first, wherever you go, and however the day went, you carry this with you. This can be good, but it's most often bad. And second, because you carry this with you when you come home your physical body is home, but you're still

at work. And when you go to work your physical body is at the office, but you're still at home. Wherever you go, you're never really *there*. You're always somewhere else.

If you had a rough day at the office, if you're not careful then when you walk in through the door of your home you'll carry that frustration with you into your home. Imagine this frustration as a cloud of energy that hangs over your head. You know the classic cartoon image where someone is walking around with a rainy cloud right above their heads? Whether it's rain or sunshine, we often carry a cloud just like this over our own head. That is, we carry our emotional energy from place to place. What we need to do is learn how to take this energy, this cloud of negative emotion, and leave it where it originated. If we can do this, we'll discover that this emotional energy isn't a part of us, but separate, and we'll be able to release the grip it has on us.

If work was frustrating, leave that frustration at work. Don't take that frustration home to your family. If you had a rough day at home during the day, don't take it into the evening, leave it where it was. Not just in another *place*, but in the *past* as well. You're in a new place in each and every moment. Even if you went to sleep at home and woke up at home, the home you woke up in is not the same home you went to bed in. Each moment is unique, and the emotional energy we typically carry with us doesn't have to carry on from moment to moment.

When we live in this way, we're never really present, we exist wherever our problems exist. When you go home, if work is where your stress and frustration exists then you'll always be distracted at home, unable to give your family your full presence. If you had a fight last night with your spouse, when you wake up in the morning you'll feel that same energy hanging over your head if you don't make the decision to become fully present for this moment. Your mind will still exist in "last night's fight". If you make the conscious decision to raise your awareness, you'll begin to see that you decide whether to continue carrying around this emotional energy from one moment to the next or not.

Many of us cause more trouble for ourselves because we carry our problems around with us from place to place. The next time you walk through a door, whether it's the door to your home, the door to your office, or the door of a friend or family member's house, wherever you just were leave that stress, frustration, and anger behind. Become fully awake to the present moment. You're not in the office any longer, you're home, and your family deserves your full presence. As you place your hands on the doorknob or handle, imagine

this energy is being ripped apart from you and left behind. And as you close the door, imagine this energy being smashed to pieces, no longer attached to you in any way. Be fully present for the act of opening the door in front of you and closing the door behind you. Don't have your phone in one hand and opening the door with the other, have both hands on the door knob or handle and open it carefully with your full presence. In that moment, you've now become fully alive. You're no longer at the office, or home, or in that fight you just had with your boss, spouse, friend, family member, or whoever else, you're fully alive right now in this moment. Whatever happened is in the past, and you have arrived in the present moment. This is a very beneficial practice and one that can help you begin to see that the emotions you feel are not you in the most real sense. We can do this at all points in the day, but two of the most beneficial times to practice this is when we retire at night and when we wake up in the morning.

Death, then Life

Upon retiring, sleep as if you had entered your last sleep. Upon awakening, leave your bed behind you instantly as if you had cast away a pair of old shoes.

- Soyen Shaku, first Zen priest to visit America

Buddhaimonia
ZEN FOR EVERYDAY LIFE

In each moment, we have a choice. We have the choice to continue living the same way we always have, attached to some past or future event, or die to both and awaken to find new life in the present moment.

When we lie down at night, we often carry our problems from that day into our time for rest. If some future event has been bothering us, something that's to come, we'll often lie down mulling over the possibilities endlessly until we fall asleep. And once we're asleep, we can even dream about those same worries. Both of these things have a substantial effect on the quality of our sleep, which extends out to every other area of our lives.

Carrying our problems around with us is only natural. We want to figure out a solution to them so that we don't have to be bothered by them any longer, but if we consistently hold onto them and never give ourselves any rest then all we end up doing is torturing ourselves. And if you take a second to think back, anything you've worried about before in your life has almost never turned out as bad as you imagined it would. We let things sit in our mind for so long that we magnify them to the point where they become monsters. And then when they actually come to be, they end up being nothing like we had imagined.

Buddhaimonia
ZEN FOR EVERYDAY LIFE

When you go to sleep tonight, right as soon as you enter your bedroom, take a moment and imagine yourself gathering up all of your problems and all of the events of the past day and placing them into a big bag, like the one Santa Claus carries around on Christmas. Once you've placed everything into your bag, place the bag down on the ground outside of your room. As you lie down for bed, there's no past and no future. There's nothing but this moment, and in this moment you're laying down to rest. You're not regretting something that happened last week, you're not down about earlier today, you're not worried about tomorrow, and not stressing about next week. All of those things are in your bag. There's literally nothing, not even the good stuff, in your mind. Good and bad, suffering and peace, are two sides of the very same coin.

Years ago, on a typical night, to think about my son before bed would also be to think about the rent payment I'm late on. If I thought about one, the likelihood is I'd think about the other. At the end of the day, everything has a way of coming back to you in a nice neat little package. So when you lay down, you place everything aside, not just the bad stuff. In this moment, you die to the past, future, and your imagination completely. Everything is thrown away and your old body and mind is discarded. You exist wholly in each new moment, unburdened by past chains. Lie down to rest tonight a fresh new you, free and at peace.

When you rise in the morning, you should do much the same. When you wake up in the morning following a rough day, in a very literal sense all the worries and problems of yesterday are in the past, so you should treat them as such. You've now begun a fresh new 24 hours and this blessing is something you should take full advantage of.

When you first wake up, if you don't do anything about it, you'll just go back to thinking about your problems. To combat this, when you wake up you should leave your bed *immediately* and become fully present for this wonderful morning. You can say this to yourself upon waking to set the tone of your day:

I have arrived.

These new 24 hours are a gift which I will cherish.

And I will make the most of each new moment presented to me.

When you say "I have arrived", imagine yourself instantly becoming fully awake to this moment. With the second line, reflect on the incredible gift that a new 24 hours is. And with the

Buddhaimonia
ZEN FOR EVERYDAY LIFE

last line, vow to make the most of the present moment throughout your day. When you wake up, you're walking through the door of today and leaving behind yesterday. Cast away your bed and all the baggage of yesterday that goes with it as if you're never going to see it again. If you can learn to do this you'll be able loosen the stranglehold that past and future events have on your mind, making it all that much easier to exist more fully in the peace of the present moment.

At times, exercises like this can seem like nonsense. "So I imagine my problems going away and that's supposed to actually make them go away? Right." But remember, our past regrets and future worries exist only in our minds. The only truth is in this moment, anything else is a projection of our minds, a mental recreation of past events or an imagination of future possibilities. These recollections and imaginations are skewed visions of our true past experience or often exaggerated ideas of our potential future experiences. They're both altered based on our wrong views and don't represent true reality. The only thing that truly exists is this moment. Exist fully in the *now* and all wrong views and perceptions disappear. In order to overcome your stress and anxiety you need to learn how to die and find new life in each moment. No matter where you go, be there, and let go of the rest.

Buddhaimonia
ZEN FOR EVERYDAY LIFE

Stopping

Wherever you are, you can go back to yourself. You're never truly lost as long as you have your breath.

In Buddhism, spiritual practice can, in a way, be separated into two aspects: acquiring both calmness and clarity of mind. Both aspects go towards the same one goal of obtaining greater awakening, or enlightenment, though so they should be looked at as two sides of the same coin rather than two separate things.

Samatha, a Sanskrit word which translates directly as "stopping", is the act of stopping, calming, resting, and healing the mind. I think the direct translation of samatha, whether intentional or not, gets straight to the point: we need to learn how to stop (or calm) our minds. And it isn't enough just to sit down and do something that feels peaceful, like reading a book or getting a spa treatment. These are temporary and general feel-

goods that don't get to the heart of it. Sure, they help, but we need more than just a peaceful hour every couple of weeks. We need a daily practice. A practice *which is meant to serve our entire being*. This is the daily practice which *Zen for Everyday Life* is about, and learning the art of stopping is an important part of that.

Going Home

At Plum Village, Zen master Thich Nhat Hanh's monastery in France, a bell sounds at various moments in the day. The bell is used to notify the monks, nuns, and lay visitors of important events such as the beginning of meditation sessions, dharma talks (Buddhist lectures), and meal time. But it's also used for another reason. Any time the bell sounds, literally every waking soul at Plum Village stops. They all just...stop. And in that moment, while the bell sounds, they practice mindful breathing. Every monk, nun, and layperson breathes in with mindfulness and breathes out with mindfulness. This is the practice of 'Going Home', and it's the practice of reuniting mind and body, the practice of finding peace by bringing our awareness inward.

To go home to yourself, all you have to do is stop and follow your breath. The beauty of this

Buddhaimonia
ZEN FOR EVERYDAY LIFE

practice is that no matter where you are, no matter what you're doing, this is a practice you can do throughout your day. At work? Stop in front of your keyboard and follow your breath for a moment (no one will even notice). At home? Tell your husband or wife about your practice and they won't think you're weird when you become seemingly frozen for a full minute. Wherever you are, you can go back to yourself. You're never truly lost as long as you have your breath. Whenever you feel rushed, stressed, or just lost, go home. Go back to your breath and find your center again. You'll realize that you were never truly lost.

Going Home is easy, and it's a practice we can do at any time of day and in any position-standing, sitting, whatever, there's no rules as to what position your body is in, what time of day it is, or what's going on around you. You can always go home to your breath. And by turning the practice of Going Home into a daily practice we can not only help ground ourselves throughout our daily life and find greater peace, we can also further support our practice of developing greater awareness as a daily habit. To do this, we'll create our very own "Bell of Mindfulness", just like the one at Plum village:

🌀 ***Set an alarm.*** Set an alarm to go off every hour, or longer if you prefer. I prefer to use a bell sound to make it feel like I'm at my very own temple, surrounded by a sense of peace, joy, and fortitude. I have an alarm on my smartphone set to go off once every hour of every day, from about 8 A.M. to 8 P.M. Plan to practice mindful breathing for about one minute every time the alarm goes off. And don't accept any excuses from yourself. It's just sixty seconds, so it should be easy to fit into your day no matter how busy you are.

🌀 ***Breathe mindfully.*** Every time my reminder goes off I imagine the bell sounding at my temple and, no matter where I am, I'm transported to a place of peace and quiet. When this bell sounds, everything stops. I don't listen to the excuses I try to give myself about "I'm almost done, let me just finish this one thing", or "I'll get to it in just a minute". I stop everything and just breathe mindfully. No matter where I am or what I'm doing, I stop. If I'm not comfortable I immediately go somewhere that I am. This is your time. No matter where you are, for one minute every hour you're transported to a place of pure peace. And yet, you've never left. The peace of the present moment isn't out there- *it's in you.*

Use the bell of mindfulness to ground yourself to the present moment and find peace, joy, and relaxation in each and every day.

The Tree of Life

The next technique takes another direction with mindful breathing. Remember that when we sit to meditate in zazen that our abdomen should be relaxed to help improve our breathing. Well, we can take this one step further by not only breathing from our abdomen but also placing our attention on our abdomen as we breath. If we're put in a tough situation- we fight with a loved one or become overwhelmed and feel like we're going to pop from stress- we can use our mindful breathing to calm our minds, bring our heart rate down, and take control of the situation.

To do this technique, just begin your breathing, but this time focus on breathing heavily from your abdomen. While you breathe imagine that you are a thick tree, heavy and unbreakable. All of your focus should be on your abdomen and you should imagine yourself strongly rooted to the ground. Whatever is affecting you in this moment

can't knock you down, it can only ruffle your leaves. And like a strong wind, with time, it dissipates and ceases to exist. As you breathe through your abdomen imagine that your anger or stress is gradually calming, as the wind that attempts to blow the tree down eventually calms. Breath is life, and as long as you're mindful of your breathing you are fully alive and standing tall.

To further enhance this practice you can take a seat, preferably in the lotus position. When we're standing, we tend to sway slightly, and we can be knocked down. But when we're sitting, especially in the lotus position, we're extremely stable and can't be knocked down. This will give you an additional sense of stability. Use this technique any time you find yourself in a tough spot.

Smiling

Sometimes, you should smile just because.

At first, this might not seem very Zen. A smile has nothing to do with being present, or with piercing through to the heart of reality in order to find peace of mind, or has anything to do with expressing our true nature. But what a smile does, and does exceptionally well, is release the tension, stress, and help relieve the anger we often unknowingly carry on our faces throughout each day as a result of our everyday life.

If, in the beginning at least, we need to wash away the tension, stress, and any lingering negative emotions in order to progress, then a smile is an amazing tool to assist in that purpose. We carry around so much tension on our faces, and worst of all, we don't notice it. Adopting a simple "half-smile" will immediately make you aware of, and remove, all of the tension in your face. In fact, after practicing a half-smile, you might notice that

Buddhaimonia
ZEN FOR EVERYDAY LIFE

all or most of the stress you're feeling dissipates after you smile. We often hold stress inside of our bodies, and by adopting the proper physical postures or positions and simply relaxing from time to time we can relieve much of that stress and tension. The half-smile is a great example of a tool which allows you to do that.

What is a half-smile? Have you ever seen a statue of the Buddha? Not the fat one (typically representative of "Maitreya", the "future" Buddha), but the typically slender man sitting in meditation with some specific hand positioning. That's "the" Buddha, born Siddhārtha Gautama. Ever noticed his subtle smile? That's a half-smile. I know, you're secretly glad that I'm not asking you to plaster your cheeks to your temples.

All you need to do is form a light smile by raising your cheeks ever-so-slightly, maybe a centimeter, or an inch at most. When you do this, you'll notice your face will immediately release all of the tension held within it. The first few times you do this exercise, really paying attention to how the half-smile relaxes the tension in your face, it can be pretty surprising. It's almost unbelievable just how much tension we typically hold in our faces. And this same principle extends to the rest of our bodies, as we'll discuss in the last chapter of Part II (*Resting*).

How to Use the Half-Smile

So, how and where exactly do you use a half-smile? Anywhere and anyhow really, but here's some specific tips:

When:

Meditation- You can adopt a half-smile while meditating, gently releasing all the stress and tension in your face before beginning your meditation session.

When feeling overwhelmed- Stressful day? Notice yourself rushing around, beginning to get overwhelmed, or just have a lot on your plate and want to stay in control? At first, it can be really difficult to keep your daily practice up, so having some techniques to quell the storm of modern life can go a long way. Form a half-smile to release, or prevent, some of that pressure.

Just because- You don't need a reason to smile. Whether you feel like smiling or not, adopting a half-smile is a rewarding practice. Sometimes, you should smile just because.

Buddhaimonia
ZEN FOR EVERYDAY LIFE

Where:

Right as you notice from the corner of your eye that a stranger is looking at you, smile really big and open your eyes wide, and then slowly move your gaze over to them. That will creep them out real good! Seriously though, there's no "place" for a smile. You can smile anywhere and at any time, so throw it into your bag of tricks as a valuable technique to use in any situation.

The Science of Smiling

Some of us roll our eyes at the thought of forcing a smile to change our mood, I know I did. But the power of a smile, whether you feel happy or joyful at the moment of smiling or not, can't be overstated. The act of smiling to change your mood is sometimes called "mouth Yoga", and it works. The brain can't tell the difference between a real smile and a fake one, so you can gain the benefits of smiling even from faking it. And the more you do it, the better you feel.

The scientific process of a smile is pretty straightforward. When you smile, endorphins are released. Endorphins are neurotransmitters which are triggered by the movements of muscles in the face. The brain then, having interpreted these

movements, releases the chemical endorphin. When endorphins are released they make us feel more pleasant and more relaxed. As a part of that process, when endorphins are increased, the stress hormone cortisol is reduced which then lowers our stress and anxiety levels.

Don't take science's word for it though, practice a half-smile and see how it works for you. It can be a valuable tool for breaking the pattern of stress and tension in your life.

Eating

Because we know the true origin and nature of the food in front of us, we can be very grateful for it.

On a typical day, I'll eat breakfast somewhere around 8 A.M, lunch varying from 1-4 P.M., and dinner usually 6-7 P.M. With slight variance, this is a pretty typical schedule for most people. Three meals a day, morning-afternoon-night, possibly with the occasional snack as well as drinks such as coffee, tea, or water throughout the day. It goes without saying that food is a huge part of all of our lives. So, what if we could bring our practice into meal time? What if we sat and ate each meal in mindfulness and with a deep understanding and appreciation for the food placed in front of us? This could be completely transformative. You really could focus on starting your *Zen for Everyday Life* practice solely with eating and it would have a profound effect on your state of mind.

Buddhaimonia
ZEN FOR EVERYDAY LIFE

There's a number of powerful techniques we can use to make meal time a deeper and more nourishing experience. You don't have to use each and every one of the techniques I'm going to mention. It's your choice, what's most important is just that you eat deeply and with mindfulness.

First, we'll cover a very powerful practice which can be done before eating to deepen the act of consuming food and further improve your practice of mindful eating. They're the 5 food contemplations:

The 5 Food Contemplations

The 5 Food Contemplations are a simple practice that can enhance your relationship with food and deepen your daily practice, and consequently your life, as a whole. The 5 Food Contemplations are to be done right before you eat. I'll cover each point in detail here, but remember that before eating you'll just be touching on each contemplation for a moment. Even 30 seconds (total, for all five contemplations) can be very beneficial, but you can take a minute or two if you'd like to really take the practice to a different level. The 5 Food Contemplations are:

Buddhaimonia
ZEN FOR EVERYDAY LIFE

1. This food is a gift of the earth, the sky, numerous living beings, and much hard and loving work.

2. May we eat with mindfulness and gratitude so as to be worthy to receive this food.

3. May we recognize and transform unwholesome mental formations, especially our greed and learn to eat with moderation.

4. May we keep our compassion alive by eating in such a way that reduces the suffering of living beings, stops contributing to climate change, and heals and preserves our precious planet.

5. We accept this food so that we may nurture our brotherhood and sisterhood, build our Sangha, and nourish our ideal of serving all living beings.

Let's break down the 5 food contemplations a bit. I won't get too deep into them, but the more you understand about the food on your plate the deeper and more beneficial relationship you'll have with it and the world around you. As I mentioned earlier, it goes without saying that food is a huge part of our lives, which is why this practice can be very beneficial:

Buddhaimonia
ZEN FOR EVERYDAY LIFE

1. This food is a gift of the earth, the sky, numerous living beings, and much hard and loving work.

Realize both where your food comes from and what your food is "made up" of (remember our friend the orange juice?). It took a whole lot of work to get that, say, apple in the supermarket into your hands- from building the orchard, to planting the soil, to dropping the seed, to tending to the tree for years as it grows and eventually bears fruit, to continuing to tend to the tree so it produces fruit year after year until the year that it bears the exact apple that sits in your hand, to the farmer who tends to the entire orchard, to any chemicals used in growing or preserving the apple, to the factory that gathered and packaged the apple, the vehicle that transported the apple, and the supermarket that stocked the apple. Phew. It's pretty crazy when you think about it, isn't it?

Now imagine that a similar (and sometimes greater) amount of work was required to bring every single item in the supermarket within arm's reach of you to purchase, cook, and consume. And a lot of items in the supermarket come from other countries around the world: fruits, vegetables, and other items that we'd otherwise never have a chance to taste if it wasn't for this complex system of development and transportation that we've developed as a species.

But more importantly, on a deeper level, you should be aware of what your food *really* is. The apple doesn't start in the orchard as a seed, the apple existed before it was even a seed, in the soil, the sky, the grass, and in the trees. What happens to an apple core when you throw it on the ground? Eventually it decomposes and dissolves into the soil. Is the apple an apple any longer, or is it the soil? There's no need to make a distinction, to call the process something, or to have an answer. This is simple the way of things, and understanding this deeply will make the practice of eating your meal a very nourishing and joyful practice.

2. May we eat with mindfulness and gratitude so as to be worthy to receive this food.

Because we know the true origin and nature of the food in front of us, we can be very grateful for it. We should eat this food in mindfulness not just because it's important for us to do so but also as a matter of respect for the food in front of us, the journey it had to make, and a matter of respect for

all of those things which allowed the food to come to be and eventually arrive on our plate- the people, the trees, the soil, etc. There's people around the world each and every day that die of starvation, or simply go without having enough to eat. Be grateful for the food in front of you, if you understand this then each meal will become a very deep and significant practice.

3. May we recognize and transform unwholesome mental formations, especially our greed and learn to eat with moderation.

We may understand the nature of the food and what it took to get the food in front of us, but we also need to be aware of the way we consume food. Do we waste large portions of food every time we eat and cook? Most people do, so if that's you then don't think you're alone. I know my wife and I definitely did for a number of years. This is something we're still working on, but I make it a point to completely finish every plate I serve myself and we do a far better job now at staying on top of expiration dates as well as making use of everything we have at home.

This might be a difficult concept to grasp if you're living relatively comfortably, at least to

where eating every night isn't an issue, which is how I grew up, but we should eat in a way that we're respectful for the fact that others in the world don't have enough to eat. We should eat until we're full, but not stuff ourselves, over consume, waste, or in any way abuse our easy access to food and clean drinking water.

There's many ways this can manifest, but for the sake of the chapter what's important for now is just that you begin realizing the complete story of the food in front of you and grow to respect it fully. With a deep respect for the food you eat, it doesn't matter what action follows, whatever the act is, it will be one that promotes peace not only for yourself but for all other living beings.

4. May we keep our compassion alive by eating in such a way that reduces the suffering of living beings, stops contributing to climate change, and heals and preserves our precious planet.

I've been a vegetarian for somewhere around 5 years. While I became a vegetarian for other reasons, what I read years later about the U.N. urging a global shift to a vegan diet really kept me a vegetarian and got me to begin shifting to complete veganism. My family and I are slowly shifting over, we've removed our consumption of milk almost completely and have now started removing cheese from our diets, but I believe it's better to make small changes at a time, especially in the case of altering one's diet.

The reason I mention this isn't to try and get you to become or promote vegetarianism, veganism, or whatever else. I simply want you to become more aware of what you eat, how it's produced, how that production affects other people around the world, how everything you do leaves a small footprint on the rest of the world (and how the footprints of others affects *you*), and how that can manifest itself. If all you do is contemplate even for a short moment on this each time you eat, it will be beneficial to your life and the life of those around you.

5. We accept this food so that we may nurture our brotherhood and sisterhood, build our Sangha, and nourish our ideal of serving all living beings.

Buddhist monks would traditionally (and still do, in some countries) receive offerings of food and other supplies from laymen and laywomen

Buddhaimonia
ZEN FOR EVERYDAY LIFE

(essentially non-monk or nun practitioners, living "normal" lives). In accord with living with greater awareness, monks and nuns would stay keenly aware of the purpose for which they would receive these offerings.

This point might seem like it doesn't apply to someone leading a more "normal", or modern, life but it's an important point to contemplate even for someone not living as a monk or nun. Let's reword it slightly to fit the modern man or woman:

I accept this food so that I may nurture my brotherhood and sisterhood (the people in my community), build my Sangha (community), and serve all living beings.

A sangha is a community of practitioners in a Buddhist monastery, as well as the entire community of living and non-living beings at large- all sentient beings that exist. Each person has many different sanghas- your direct family, extended family and friends, greater community, country, the world, and even the universe. Ultimately there's just one Sangha, the Sangha which includes all sentient beings, which is the universal Sangha, but it helps to look at your life as a series of "sub-sanghas", if you will.

The Sangha is your community, the community with which you share your life. Once you realize your own interbeing with all other living and non-living things you realize a deep sense of meaning in your life. People search their entire lives for a sense of meaning and never find it. The problem a lot of people make is that they continually search within themselves, never expanding their awareness to the world around them (reality). When you begin feeling your connection with the rest of the world, you naturally act in a way that you not just improve your own well-being, but also improve the well-being as well as protect the livelihood of all other living and non-living things.

So, take this realization and apply it to our reworded contemplation. In Zen, it's understood that life is a dance between gift, giver, and receiver. In any moment, you're giving, receiving, and the gift itself all at the same time. Being aware of your interbeing, you should do your part to contribute to the betterment of the world at large and appreciate the effort of all those living and non-living things which contributed to the creation, development, transportation, and sale of the food in front of you. *This fifth contemplation is about making the commitment to do your part to contribute to the greater well-being of the world at large.* Before you eat your meal, contemplate for a moment on this. We each have a part in making this world a better place, and while the meal in front of you might just seem like "just another dinner", when you look a little deeper, it's anything but that.

———————————

The 5 Food Contemplations can be done for a few seconds, or even a few minutes, before and after you eat. Take just a moment to contemplate on each of the 5 contemplations and watch as your relationship with food deepens and helps bring peace and joy to your life.

Eating Meditation

Eating with mindfulness is the centerpiece of this chapter. Eating with mindfulness, as with any of the other mindfulness practices discussed in this book, grounds you to the present reality and brings you greater mental clarity and peace of mind.

As we talked about earlier, mindfulness is always grounded by a central point of attention, and always of something that you yourself are doing (listening, seeing, breathing, walking, eating), and this makes it easy to know how to practice mindfulness in any situation. So what is our object of meditation here? Primarily, the act of chewing. You need simply be mindful of the act of placing the food in your mouth and of chewing and swallowing the food. Zen Buddhist monks and nuns chew each bite at least 30 times to enhance their practice, but they're also aware that it aids in digestion, which is a nice bonus (also, chewing this many times, as well as eating with mindfulness, makes you eat slower which typically curbs overeating).

Chew the food in your mouth with all of your being. While you're chewing, nothing else matters more. And this includes the next bite. Don't chew your food while picking up your utensil and preparing another bite. Pick up your fork, spoon, chop sticks or whatever you're using, place the bite in your mouth, and place your hand down on the table (with utensil in hand or not, either way) so that you can put your absolute focus on the bite in your mouth. And as always, gently acknowledge whatever various thoughts and sensations come to your mind while eating, don't push them away. You're the silent observer of all that occurs within your field of awareness, not just the act of chewing.

Depending on where you eat, what meal it is, and who is eating with you, this can be difficult at times (imagine two kids!). Just do your best and take it one step at a time. And remember that you can eat with a relaxed awareness if need be (level 2).

Buddhaimonia
ZEN FOR EVERYDAY LIFE

Silent Eating

Zen monks and nuns typically eat in absolute silence. The purpose of this is to further deepen your mindfulness practice and support an all-around peaceful atmosphere. There's not much I can say about this except- try it. It will be weird at first if you're doing it with someone else, but you and whoever you're sitting with will quickly realize how beneficial it is to sit and practice mindful eating in silence.

After the meal is done, you can choose to continue sitting and have a mindful conversation with the other person or persons (if you're not eating alone) or simply get up and finish the meal. It's nice to not jump right up after eating and run off. This won't always be possible, but when it is, take advantage of it.

Buddha-Food

To further deepen your practice, you can take a moment to observe the true nature of an apple. Take a moment to look deeply into the apple and see that the apple is really made up of all non-apple elements. The clouds in the sky that turned to rain, the soil in the ground that provided the tree nutrients to grow, the tree that transferred those

nutrients to each apple on the tree from its roots all the way up to the end of its branches, and fthe farmer that had to farm the apple in order for it to get to you. And if you were to take away even one of these elements, the apple would cease to exist.

This apple is a product of the entire cosmos, and when you eat this apple, you eat the cosmos itself. This practice can help you to begin see everything else in a similar manner. The apple isn't an exception, everything around you is the same way. You're made up of the elements of exploding stars light-years away. You're made up of the same basic building blocks as everything else around you, and those things you see as separate from you, such as the clouds, trees, and mountains, are intrinsically connected to you. Think about that for a moment. How wonderful life is when you take a moment to look deeply into the typical things you do in your everyday life.

Cooking the Buddha

I'd like to end with a few quick notes on cooking and preparing food. Eating isn't the only place that allows you to be mindful of food, cooking and preparing food in mindfulness is also a nourishing practice.

When you cook or prepare food, as you gather your ingredients, lay them out, cut them up, and put them wherever they need to go (a pot, pan, stove), be mindful of exactly what you're doing in that very moment. You're not cooking food to be eaten, you're simply cooking the food, and you're doing it will all of your being. If you think that you're cooking the food in order to eat it then you're already dispersing your awareness and not being completely present for this moment. Cook simply with the intention of cooking, and cook with your whole being as if this is the most important thing you will ever do.

Driving

Break the cycle now and decide, "I'm here, right now, alive in this moment. I'm not driving to get somewhere. I'm simply driving, and driving with my whole being."

In the truest sense, in every moment we're both living and dying. But in every moment we have the choice to either live life fully awake, or to live in a way that we're simply walking towards our own death unaware of the beauty of life all around us. We're so inclined to live life always thinking about the future, "what do I have to do next week?", "I'm worried about what might happen tomorrow", "what's going to happen in the future?" And even if we're not particularly worried about anything, we still live most of our lives in the future, from making plans to predicting outcomes.

What we don't notice is, when we live in this way, we're driving to our deaths. Imagine you're in a car, whatever car you want to imagine yourself in (go wild). Now imagine you're driving that car on a large stretch of highway. This highway extends so far out, and perfectly straight, that you can't really see the end of it. The way we usually live, we're racing down this highway, looking at the end of the road, and trying to get to the end as quickly as possible. But every few feet we speed past, a beautiful landmark blows past us, never to be seen again. You see, there's no reverse on this highway. You can only stop and go. If you look back, what you see is only a broken image of reality, and you can never again see the landmark because it no longer exists. So off you go, passing up landmark after landmark, so focused on moving forward that you're blowing past all of the most beautiful moments of your life. And the end of the road? The end of your life.

Each of these landmarks is a moment in the present reality. Each and every moment is beautiful and profound, and the more we stay locked away in our minds the less alive we really are. Looking to the future is OK, making plans is necessary, but we should live grounded in the present reality. Remember this when you're driving down the highway of your life.

You might think that driving is different from this example, but it's not. Every time you get in your car, if you're not mindful, you're just getting caught up in the same mindless race.

Moving to get somewhere, so that you can go somewhere else, and go somewhere else. Going to the store, so that you can go home and cook dinner, so that you can eat and satisfy your hunger, so that you can keep working or plan for what you have to do tomorrow. All the while never actually getting to where you're going, because as soon as you get there you're already working on getting somewhere else. Break the cycle now and decide, "I'm here, right now, alive in this moment. I'm not driving to get somewhere, I'm simply driving, and driving with my whole being." Feel yourself become fully present for the driving experience.

Each time you step into your car, say to yourself:

As I step into this car,
I take refuge in the present moment.

I have nowhere to go, and no one to see,
I drive like an eagle soaring through the sky,
Free-flying, and clear-minded.

Unbound by past and future,
I exist fully in the peace of the present moment.

Buddhaimonia
ZEN FOR EVERYDAY LIFE

Driving is a bit different from every other activity we've discussed thus far. It's more of a set of activities than it is one single activity. Sitting at a red light presents the ideal opportunity to stop and follow your breath, driving presents the opportunity to be mindful of your hands on the wheel, and simply being alone presents the opportunity to contemplate, or you could even have a silent drive.

Dharma Talk Time

I admittedly split my driving time into two parts: part driving meditation and part listening to audiobooks. Being a father, husband, and running my business all take up a lot of my time, so the couple of hours I'm in my car every week are perfect for listening to audiobooks. I like to consider this my "dharma talk time" (dharma in this case referring to "teachings on the way it is/the nature of reality", and dharma talk referring to Buddhist lectures). As I turn on my audio, I imagine myself walking into a temple to listen to my favorite Zen teachers speak.

The silence you get while driving by yourself in your car is a valuable time to do a number of things. It's the perfect time to absorb information

Buddhaimonia
ZEN FOR EVERYDAY LIFE

because you are, for the most part, alone and uninterrupted. Being alone in my car, I can not only listen to an audiobook with rather undivided attention, I can contemplate on the material being discussed. I listen to and read all kinds of books, but I center around books on Zen, so as you can imagine sometimes I just need to hit "pause" and let what was just discussed sit with me for a while.

No matter what type of book you decide to listen to, preferably a book that imparts wisdom, if you decide to do the same then as you get in your car and get ready to turn your car on, imagine yourself walking into a beautiful building. This building is empty, except for you, and the author. It's just the two of you sitting in this big room, and he or she is reading their book to you line by line as if it were a speech or story made for you.

Also, I have to say, I haven't delved into why but I absorb the information in an audiobook much better than I do reading a traditional book, even when I take notes as I read. This is a very important point to mention. You can read all you want, but if you're only retaining 10% of what you're reading then it'll take a whole lot of reading to get any sort of significant benefit.

Driving Meditation

Buddhaimonia
ZEN FOR EVERYDAY LIFE

As I mentioned earlier, driving is a little different from every other activity in this section. Driving meditation is really split into two parts: the act of driving itself and being stopped at a red light or in heavy traffic.

When driving, it can be difficult to know what to place your concentration on. Should you be mindful of your foot on the pedal, of your hands on the wheel, or your eyes on the road? You can really be mindful of any of those things, but I've found that, at least for me, it's easiest to focus my attention on my hands steering the car. This is especially effective because of all the "micro-turns" you have to make while driving. That is, the slight adjustments of the wheel you have to make, especially when driving fast on the freeway and constantly turning slightly here and there. The wheel never actually sits still, so it's a really effective spot to place your attention.

Keep in mind though that driving meditation is essentially always done with a relaxed awareness, the second level of awareness, because you can't possibly just focus your attention on your hands when your foot is constantly going up and down on the pedal, lights are turning colors, cars are switching lanes around you, and you're constantly turning left and right. Drive with the second level of awareness and driving

meditation becomes a beautifully grounding practice.

I know you probably don't keep both hands on the wheel in the position your high school driving instructor taught you, but that's the best position for driving meditation. You want to be fully engaged in the driving experience, so place both of your hands near the top of the wheel, separated a bit less than shoulder distance apart. The next part is simple, place your attention on your hands on the wheel and be mindful of all the other various sensations that arise while driving. Know that you're here right now driving this car. Be aware that you're driving *to* somewhere, but being mindful of the drive itself, you're grounded in the present moment "simply driving".

So, you hit a stop light. What do you do now? We already covered the difficult part, now it's easy: when you stop, simply become mindful of your breath. Any time you see a red light it should be a reminder to stop and go back to your breath (use the same instructions we used in the *Stopping* chapter). Be mindful of your in-breath and out-breath, and make sure to keep your eyes up so that you can see the light in your peripheral vision. Of course, you don't have to keep your eyes up, but be prepared to get honked at when you're sitting there in silence and everyone behind you is freaking out because the light is green and they have

Buddhaimonia
ZEN FOR EVERYDAY LIFE

"somewhere" to go. So yeah, better keep your eyes up.

Anytime you have the opportunity to stop and follow your breath is a beautiful moment, and driving allows many opportunities for that. Red lights really will start to take on a different meaning. I didn't exactly hate red lights before (some people *really* hate them), but I disliked them because it meant I was going to take longer to get to wherever I was going. Now, I love red lights and welcome the moment to stop and simply follow my breath.

Use driving meditation to put a stop to the constant "go, go, go" of the day and make a statement: I'm not going to rush around any longer. I'm here, fully present for the beauty that this day holds.

A Silent Drive

When you're driving alone, it can already be a really peaceful experience. But have you ever tried turning *off* the radio, rolling up the windows, ignoring your phone even at stop lights, clearing your mind, and driving in absolute silence? This is what I simply call a "silent drive".

So, let's do just that:

Buddhaimonia
ZEN FOR EVERYDAY LIFE

🌀 *Turn off the radio.* You might think music will enhance the experience, but for the most part it's just distracting and pulls control of your emotions from you. I'm mostly talking about music with singing, because it's the words and emotions they carry that are what is really distracting. Some peaceful instrumental music can at times be nice, but I'd suggest trying your drive a few times in silence first so that you know the difference.

🌀 *Roll up the windows.* This is optional, but the point is silence so it's more beneficial at first if you do this with the windows rolled up.

🌀 *Ignore your phone.* Turn it on vibrate, ignore all calls, and don't pick it up even when you stop at a stop light (not even Bluetooth!).

🌀 *Clear your mind.* "Move aside" the stress, difficulties, and projects of the day. I know it can be hard to get things out of your mind at times, so tell yourself that it's OK for you to come back to them, just at a later time (after your drive, for instance). For the time being at least, clear your mind.

🌀 *Simply drive.* Now, just drive. A silent drive will greatly enhance your driving meditation practice and make driving an incredibly peaceful and refreshing experience.

With these practices, you'll never look at driving the same way again. What was once just a way to get from point A to point B has now become a deeply spiritual and peaceful experience with the ability to completely recharge your mind and body. And you don't have to do this by yourself. There's no reason why you can't take a friend or a loved one with you on your silent drive, or driving meditation, just make sure to have them read this chapter beforehand.

The next time you get into your car, break the cycle of "go, go, go" and make the decision to live a deeper and more meaningful life. Remember this verse:

As I step into this car,
I take refuge in the present moment.

I have nowhere to go, and no one to see.
I drive like an eagle soaring through the sky,
Free-flying, and clear-minded.

Unbound by past and future,
I exist fully in the peace of the present moment.

Buddhaimonia
ZEN FOR EVERYDAY LIFE

Resting

...the energy of mindfulness has the ability to relieve much of the stress that builds up within our body.

One of the most attractive parts of a daily "spiritual" practice, most specifically meditation, as well as the aspect that should be focused on in the beginning is finding tranquility, or calm, within yourself. To do this means to quiet the internal chatter of the mind and to be able to rest in peace as a pebble rests at the bottom of a pond.

The major tool in accomplishing this is indeed meditation, as sleep is often hardly an opportunity for total relaxation- the constant tossing and turning, with dreams frequently disrupting your otherwise quiet state of mind. It doesn't by itself provide for us the level of peace and relaxation that we need to operate at our best or allow us to go beyond a simple calmness of mind. But nonetheless, it plays an important role in your overall well-being and ability to achieve

Buddhaimonia
ZEN FOR EVERYDAY LIFE

peace of mind, so learning how to make the most of your time for rest is important (especially for those with trouble sleeping).

You can greatly improve the quality of your sleep, and therefore help your mind and body find greater peace and relaxation, by making a few simple changes to your nightly routine. We spoke earlier in the chapter on *Arriving* about the practice of being fully present in the moment of going to bed, putting the worries of the day aside, and fully committing to the act of resting. This is a great technique that you can use to improve the quality of your sleep and bring peace to your day. But we can take it one step further by using our greater awareness as a form of healing energy.

The Healing Energy of Awareness

In any given moment, our attention is splintered in countless directions. This is due to the mind's desire to constantly stay ahead. We've become naturally conditioned to keeping multiple things in our mind at a time so that we don't lose control of our illusory hold on reality. It's because of this that in the beginning of our practice our minds are all over the place. We never want to let anything go for fear that everything will fall apart.

Buddhaimonia
ZEN FOR EVERYDAY LIFE

But it's only in letting go that we're able to find peace and calm. Two important points here:

🌀 First, by holding onto our problems and worries, and consequently stacking up so much stress and anxiety, we actually do physical damage to our bodies. It's no secret that stress affects more than just our minds, stress has been shown to have a sort of "global" effect on the body- that is, it can affect the entire body and mind equally and heavily for that matter- but most of the time we're not completely in touch with exactly what is causing our stress. We have an idea, and sometimes we blame certain things, but oftentimes we don't hit the nail on the head. Either that, or we're way off.

🌀 Second, because of our unfamiliarity with living in a state of complete awareness, when we do then begin practicing mindfulness the effects on our mind and body can seem almost magical in nature. But less so than having a magical effect, mindfulness simply returns us to our natural expression, and therefore takes apart the stress machine that exists within our minds and uncovers a peaceful state of being that nourishes us instead of breaking us down, for however long we're being mindful. This can then be taken however far you'd like- for half a day, two hours, or simply fifteen minutes daily- and you'll reap proportionate rewards as a byproduct.

One clear example of the power of mindfulness' ability to break down this physically threatening stress machine is in the practice of "scanning" your body with your mindfulness. To do this, as soon as you lie down for bed, and preferably after you do the nightly exercises described in the *Death, then Life* section of the *Arriving* chapter, pick a point on your body. It can be wherever, but it will probably be easier to keep track if you pick the top of your head or your toes (the top or bottom of your body).

Let's say you started with your head. Imagine your physical brain and feel whatever sensations you can in and around your head with your mindfulness. Your absolute awareness is concentrated on the top of your head and nowhere else. The purpose of this exercise is to "direct" your mindful awareness to each area of your body and send your love, gratitude, and attention to each area. Do this for a minute or two on each area of your body, moving along your body in sequence. In

this case from your head, to your face, to your neck, to your shoulders, and so on.

This might sound odd, but let's take your face for example. Remember the chapter on *Smiling*? Many of us can go an entire day without smiling more than a handful of times, if at all, and so the fact that our faces are tensed for such long periods builds up a lot stress in and around our facial muscles. Simply becoming aware of this brings much needed relief (just as becoming mindful of your breathing, without seeking to control it, stabilizes it and consequently calms you) as becoming aware of this naturally makes us release much of this tension, and a smile changes everything, immediately bringing great relief to all the muscles in your face. That's essentially what we're doing here, but extending it to your entire body. For the most part, we're not moving our bodies because our complete awareness is enough to bring relief, but if you're focusing on, say, your toes then you can give them a little wiggle in the beginning to heighten your awareness of them and therefore improve the exercise.

This potent energy, the energy of mindfulness, has the ability to relieve much of the stress that builds up within our body. Just directing your attention to an area of your body naturally relaxes that area, and so by taking a few minutes to focus your mindfulness on each area of

Buddhaimonia
ZEN FOR EVERYDAY LIFE

your body you can create a great amount of relief across your entire body.

Continue moving down your body, from your shoulders down to your biceps, triceps, forearms, hands and fingers. Next, shift over to your chest and abdomen and then from your back down to that part of your body that you're probably sitting on for a rather unhealthy amount of hours each day (as millions, maybe even billions of people at this point, around the world do every single day). Then continue down to your hips, upper legs, knees, calves, feet, and finally finishing with your toes. This entire exercise can take up to 20-30 minutes if you really take your time, but if you'd like to start at five to ten minutes in the beginning you can shorten each body part down to between 30 or 45 seconds.

By the time you've completed the exercise your body will feel completely different. That is, if you actually complete it. Most of the time your body will become so relaxed that you'll fall asleep before you can even finish the exercise. But if you *do* happen to complete the exercise, you'll feel the difference in your level of relaxation and often be well on your way to falling asleep (which is part of the point of laying down). This exercise can greatly improve the quality of your sleep and act as a nice nightly meditation. You don't have to reserve it for your night's rest though, you can use this

technique whenever you feel like. But be careful, if it's during the day I'd suggest just sitting in zazen, as laying down often prompts you to fall asleep (which is why it's perfect to do right before bed to improve the quality of your sleep), so you'll have a more productive session simply doing zazen or another practice at any other point in the day.

Nightly Tea Meditation

If the mindfulness of body exercise isn't your cup of tea (sorry, couldn't resist...), you can always try some nice, warm, and soothing tea. But don't just make some tea and drink it before bed- although a warm and soothing form of tea like a chamomile *can* help improve the quality of your sleep- you should drink the tea fully alive to each raise and lower of the arms and each sip of the tea in mindfulness and make it a calming tea meditation.

I don't usually drink tea before bed, but I drink tea pretty often, and I do a simple morning tea meditation nearly every day. It's the same idea no matter when you do it:

🌀 **Make your tea.** First, remember to stay in mindfulness from start to finish preparing

your tea- from taking out your cup, to heating your water, and sifting the tea.

🌀 **Sit.** Find a nice quiet place for you to sit and drink your tea, preferably in your room and maybe even on your bed, so that you can place the tea on your nightstand and lay down as soon as you're finished.

🌀 **Give thanks.** Before I begin drinking my tea, I place my tea down beside me, put my hands together, and simply give thanks for the cup of tea in front of me. I think of all those who don't even have access to clean drinking water, let alone a warm cup of tea, and give my gratitude and appreciation for the cup in front of me. I let myself sit in those feelings of gratitude and appreciation for a minute before moving forward.

🌀 **Drink your tea.** Next, the main event. Simply pick up your tea in mindfulness, raise your arms fully aware that you're raising your arms in this moment, and take a small sip of tea in mindfulness. Drink slowly, staying mindful the entire time. While drinking, my awareness often shifts. I often do this sequence: raise (arm), sip, swallow, lower (arm), and breathe. I take a few full breaths before raising my arms again and taking another sip of tea. Make sure to fully commit when you're doing something with your full awareness. By that I mean, for instance, drink with both of your hands holding the cup of tea. You're not reading a magazine, watching T.V., or on your phone or laptop. You're just drinking your tea with your whole being.

🌀 **Give thanks (again).** Give thanks for the tea once more before finishing and laying down for the night.

This will likely take you somewhere between 10-20 minutes if you take your time. And don't worry about finishing your tea or anything. If 20 minutes have passed and you've only finished half of your cup, that's not a problem, you've had a great tea meditation session. You can keep going and finish your session, or choose to drink the rest of your tea and go to bed.

PART III: Making Peace

Communicating

...if you want to get through to people then you have to come from a place of love, compassion, and understanding.

It's attractive to think that you can live your life in peace without ever talking to another human being, or at least to those you don't all that much care for. But in order to find true peace and happiness you need to learn how to live with others. This includes communicating- both speaking and listening to others-, loving – knowing how to be there for your loved ones, and healing- knowing how to heal the wounds that inevitably arise from time to time in any relationship. Children also bring a whole new dynamic to life and provide all kinds of new and different challenges as well. And the process of giving and receiving is the very fabric of our nature. *Making Peace* covers each of these areas.

Buddhaimonia
ZEN FOR EVERYDAY LIFE

Our peace and happiness is intrinsically linked to others. This is because, contrary to our normal everyday experience, we're not separate "things" but the whole body of the cosmos being reflected in a single expression of itself, in much the same way that a group of water droplets can all reflect the same image. Each expression is a person, and each person perfectly expresses the true nature of life itself in its entirety. If you contemplate this deeply, you begin to see that the problems, challenges, and stresses we all experience are very much the same.

These struggles we experience are a part of life for each and every one of us. Knowing this can help you develop compassion and understanding for yourself, your loved ones, as well as those you otherwise wouldn't care for. And likewise, the path to overcoming those struggles exists in one and the same place. This allows us to look within ourselves for a common answer. And that common answer is always for us to come together in peace, as opposed to fighting with one another.

Speaking Mindfully

I read a story recently about a group of researchers who had tried for years to study a specific group of gorillas in a nearby jungle. For over a decade, the gorillas wouldn't let anyone near their jungle habitat. One research team after another would make plans, test their equipment, gear up, grab guns, and set out to hopefully get close enough to study the family of gorillas...only to be pushed back by the gorillas, one research team after another.

That changed when a certain researcher decided to travel to the camp without any guns or other weapons. This researcher took a team to the very same gorilla camp that research teams had tried to visit for years and was welcomed by the gorillas with open arms. The gorillas didn't just let them stay close enough to camp out and research the gorillas, they let them stay within their very camp.

The purpose of this story is that if you want to get through to people, you can't come at them with hostility, *you have to come from a place of love, compassion, and understanding.* Any level of hostility can be felt by people (and all animals), and it will make them push back. Even if what you're saying is the truth, if it's hurtful then the other person will shut down. This is the Buddha's "Right Speech". To say something you know could be hurtful to someone is never OK, and it's never the right way to go about things, even if it's the truth. We need to always speak from a place of love and compassion.

Buddhaimonia
ZEN FOR EVERYDAY LIFE

My oldest son is 3, coming on 4, so he's at the point where he can hold a normal conversation. If he does something wrong, and I need to discipline him and explain to him why what he did wasn't OK, the only way for me to do that is with love, compassion, and understanding. Any less and he reads it, he feels my energy, and he reacts like a mirror. Adults have a few more walls built up than the average child, but we all work essentially the same way. Speak to people with love and compassion and you'll have the ability to get through to them. Be a hard ass all you want, but by coming at people with hostility and aggressiveness they'll never truly let you in.

In your own life this could mean explaining to someone your difference of opinion in a way that respects them and doesn't put them down. This could mean learning to breathe when you get angry before you even utter a word so that you don't say something you'll regret or which you know could possibly cause harm. This could also come in the form of speaking to others about things that actually take them into account, instead of giving general advice that you yourself would want to hear.

The Buddha was believed to be a master at communicating to others from the view point of their own tradition. Instead of putting others down or arguing with them as to who was "right", he understood the futility in this and instead helped others to uncover the truth through their own system of tradition (after all, the Buddha wasn't trying to get people to convert to a new religion, he simply wanted them to uncover the truth of this life we all live in, which we can and should all do through our own unique traditions and experience).

"Think before you speak" might be an old and tired saying, but it's not without merit. Before speaking, consider if what you're about to say is beneficial to the other person, if it will accomplish the desired goal, or if it can cause harm to the other person and then decide whether to speak, alter your words, or simply stay silent. Silence is also an important aspect of mindful speech to keep in mind. A moment of silence between two beats in a song isn't empty, it can be just as significant as the beats themselves. We don't always have to say something, sometimes silence is the most powerful form of communication.

Your words can destroy relationships, open wounds, transmit love, and raise people up. Speak fully aware of the conversation at hand, aware of how you're feeling and how those emotions can alter how you speak, and always seek to communicate with compassion and understanding.

Listening Deeply

A conversation is a pretty simple thing: there's a speaker and a listener (or listeners). We tend to forget that though, and *act* as if a conversation is just the process of two people alternating speaking to one another. This is best exemplified when we get into arguments, as both people are alternating between speaking and waiting for their next chance to speak, almost completely ignoring when the other person is talking. Another great example is being distracted while someone is talking to you, more common than ever with the advent of smartphones.

When someone is speaking to you, you should listen intently to what they're saying. Not only because you wish this from others, but because only by doing so do we really hear what the other person is saying to us.

To listen deeply is to listen with mindfulness, with your focus of attention on their words and the meaning behind them. To listen deeply, you shouldn't be doing anything else while in conversation with the other person. Get off your phone, your computer, stop watching T.V., and most importantly get out of your head. Do your best to hear their words in their pure form, without your opinions interjecting as they're talking. Focus

attentively on the other person, keeping eye contact with the other person and giving them your undivided attention. This is important because much of what we communicate is through our bodies- our eyes, our faces, and the rest of our body. By paying only half-attention to someone when they're speaking to you, say while you're looking at your phone, you'll only take in a portion of what they're really saying.

Make it a point to listen deeply to someone at least once a day in order to make it into a habit. Don't try deep listening in every conversation right from the get-go if you're not used to doing so, take it slow and let your daily practice be a constant reminder to listen attentively when others are speaking. Listening deeply has the ability to show you things you never noticed before, nourish your relationships by creating a deeper connection between you and your loved ones (and all other people), as well as to not only bring further peace to your own life but to the life of those you communicate with. Listen deeply, as if in that moment you were making a special connection with the other person, and you'll open a gateway to greater peace for yourself as well as those around you.

Sharing Life

Within learning *how* to mindfully use your words (or not use your words) and learning *how* to listen deeply, there's also the issue of deciding *when* to speak and *when* to listen.

Most of my life, I grew up holding everything in. No one around me ever said, "talk to me, tell me how you're feeling", and so I was never taught the importance of just talking to others about my problems. I never knew it was even an option, or that there was any real benefit to it. Partly because of that, I turned to writing. When I was in middle school, and later high school, I had this black book. It was actually a little menacing looking because it had no writing on the outside whatsoever and by the time I had had it for some 6 months it was so filled with papers (notes which I stuffed in between various pages), worn down, and torn up that it looked like something out of a demonic horror movie. Not to mention that I drew this symbol that I liked when I was younger, a cross between the Hindu "Om" symbol and a musical note, in red crayon on the front of the book. Not so bad right? Well, I used red crayon, which ended up vaguely resembling blood. Yeah...16 years old. Moving on...

The look of the book was a lot darker than the contents though. It wasn't necessarily dark, just personal. It was the only place I felt that I could fully open up. I still have that book to this day to serve as a reminder of the importance of this very point. One of the most important lessons I want to teach my children is to talk about their problems with others, and to be there for others when they need to talk. And one of the most important things I want to do as a parent is to always be there for them to talk to. About anything, anytime, and anywhere. I think it's so important for every person to both understand the value of this and to have at least one person with which they can open up to.

This is sharing life, and sometimes these talks are beautiful, sometimes they're dark, but talking in this way is always highly nourishing. It's one of the single most powerful medicines for the heart and mind that exists, and something you should begin practicing if you don't already. Sharing with others, and letting others know we're there for them to open up to, helps us overcome struggle, relieves and heals our hearts and minds, and strengthens relationships. Don't hold your troubles in, you'll only damage yourself in the long run. Learn to open up and let others in and witness the healing energy of communication.

Buddhaimonia
ZEN FOR EVERYDAY LIFE

Loving

Lovers don't finally meet somewhere. They're in each other all along.

- Rumi

Love was never an emotion I identified all that strongly with. I didn't have close relationships with many people, if any, growing up, and this had a strong effect on me later in life. I remember reading Deepak Chopra talk about love and thinking "what the heck is this guy talking about". It wasn't until my first son was born that I truly began to understand love. It's because of, as well as through, him that I see beautiful qualities in others and am able to much more easily cultivate compassion and love towards those in my life. And this includes people I've never met before.

The word love carries with it a lot of different connotations. You can love your spouse or girlfriend or boyfriend, your son or daughter, your mother or father, you can love to golf, and you can

Buddhaimonia
ZEN FOR EVERYDAY LIFE

love donuts (← this guy). The English language uses the word "love" way too often, most of the time meaning nothing more than "enjoy" or "really like". And then there's the separation between the love you have for that special person in your life and the love you have for your family or friends. It can be a bit confusing.

Love, in its truest form, is everything and everywhere. Those things which we love about our son or daughter or husband or wife aren't only in them, they're in all people. If you look deeply enough at those you love, and the specific qualities that you find most fascinating, you'll find that they exist throughout life. This isn't a bad thing, on the contrary is means that if you look closely enough you can expand your love to include all beings, both human and non-human beings. Love shouldn't be something you only have for a few people, it should be a feeling of deep appreciation, compassion, and caring for all people. This requires you to be able to see the goodness in others, which can at times be a difficult feat. But by meditating on compassion and love you can begin to cultivate the same feelings you have for your loved ones towards others, even towards those you've never met.

Meditating on Compassion

Meditating on love and compassion is a powerful exercise which you can apply as a regular meditation practice as you go about your daily life. You can meditate so as to direct love and compassion towards someone you're having problems with, like your spouse or a family member, someone you dislike or even hate, or direct your love and compassion to all beings in a single meditation.

When you meditate on compassion imagine the same feelings of love and compassion you feel for those closest to you, such as your son or daughter, husband or wife, or mother or father to gradually expand outward until they encompass all beings.

Much the same as with mindfulness, you can sit down and meditate on compassion as well as use this meditation in your everyday life, particularly anytime you encounter a difficult situation with someone. This meditation really just comes down to cultivating compassion and understanding for all beings (including yourself), so it can be done at just about any point in the day.

You can start by taking about a minute on each section until you feel comfortable doing more. A general suggestion would be to build up to about five minutes per section, but you can do it for

however long you'd like. There are no rules here, except to not do more than you feel you can do.

During this meditation you'll be attempting to stimulate positive feelings through various means so you'll have to test different things out to see what works best for you. Some people picture beautiful imagery, some chant simple phrases like "may they be well; may they be happy" (Or "I" instead of "they" if it's for you), but you can also just imagine the feelings swelling in your mind until you eventually expand to the next stage.

To meditate on compassion, follow these 5 steps:

🌀 *1ˢᵗ Stage:* Focus on yourself. Specifically, cultivating love for yourself. This particular stage might feel awkward if you do not already feel love for yourself. Don't worry about that, with practice you'll not just cultivate love for others but you'll cultivate that same love for yourself. Focus on feelings such as peace, calm, tranquility and happiness. Then, let those feelings turn into feelings of strength and confidence in oneself. Then finally, imagine those feelings turning into love.

⚙ **2nd** *Stage*: Think of a loved one such as a close friend or family member. Picture them in your mind vividly so that the feelings are as intense and as real as possible. This is important to do for each section. Feel your connection to them and think of what you value about them.

⚙ **3rd** *Stage*: Think of someone you know, but are not friends with, like an acquaintance at work. This person is neutral to you. You don't particularly like or dislike this person. Expand those feelings of love from the last stage to this person. Focus on the fact that they're human just like you, and that because of this they have their own problems and struggles, as well as their own strengths and positive qualities. This is the practice of understanding.

⚙ **4th** *Stage*: Think of someone you don't like, maybe you even have someone you'd consider an enemy. Now expand those feelings of love from the beginning stages to this person as well. As with the first stage, if this feels awkward, don't worry, just keep at it. Focus on the positive and try to see the good qualities in this person. Once again remind yourself that they're human and that they have their own set of struggles as well as positive qualities just like you.

✿ 5th *Stage*: First, think of all four people over again, which includes yourself, and extend those feelings of love and peace to them. Lastly, begin to expand those feelings to the other people around you such as extended family, then to your neighborhood, city, and state until it encompasses the entire world. Then finish the exercise by visualizing these same feelings expanding out indefinitely.

This practice is typically done while sitting in peace and quiet, but you can also do it as you go about your daily life. Depending on where you are and how much time you have, you might need or simply desire to shorten or modify the meditation to suit your needs. If you just argued with someone at work and need to spend the next 5 hours with them in what would otherwise be a really difficult and uncomfortable situation, you can take a second at your desk, in the restroom, or outside and simply do stage 4.

Likewise, if you catch yourself judging someone else as you go about your day you can take a second to send feelings of compassion, love, and understanding to them. Oftentimes simply *attempting* to understand why someone does something and thinking of potential possibilities for their behavior can help you cultivate compassion towards them. That's a really powerful exercise which I've used countless times to cultivate compassion and understanding towards people I've held unfavorable opinions of.

Loving Yourself

This chapter is about learning to express love and compassion for those around you, but before you can even think of expressing love and

Buddhaimonia
ZEN FOR EVERYDAY LIFE

compassion to others, you need to love yourself. With that in mind, think of love as a form of energy that brings life to all people. Without the energy of love in your life, you wouldn't survive. Love comes from many places, but if it doesn't accompany or result in a blossoming of love for yourself then you won't be able to love others back.

My favorite example of the connection between love and our self-worth is in Deepak Chopra's example of a baby. Imagine a young baby for a moment and visualize what it must be like to live as that baby. Chopra says there are two things a baby knows (or would if it had a concept of them):

- That it's loved, and
- That it's lovable

Now think of yourself. When you look at yourself through a mirror, what do you see? Do you see someone who is loved by others, as well as someone who is capable of being loved? The word lovable might throw you off, so let me explain. By lovable, I mean that when you look at yourself do you believe that someone could come to love you? Or do you just see your flaws? Do you spend most of your time beating yourself up and just can't come to believe how someone could see beauty in you?

By the time we're adults, most of us no longer believe we're lovable, and many of us no longer feel that we're truly loved by much more than our parents. The root of not loving ourselves is the belief that we're screwed up because of our flaws or faults. But what you need to realize is that everyone has flaws and everyone has faults, and what allows you to love yourself isn't whether or not you think you're perfect- an impossible goal that does nothing but damage one's self-worth- it's whether or not you accept yourself just as you are. Accept yourself and love yourself, just as you are, by meditating on compassion and living mindfully so as to bring these underlying issues to the surface, and you'll not only transform how you feel about yourself but be able to love others back in return.

Giving Your Presence

Your presence is the most important gift you can give to your loved ones. Your children, your spouse, your parents, and your close friends all deserve your full presence. So get off your phone, stop watching T.V., get your head out of the office,

and stop worrying about this and that so you can be completely present for those you love.

Our presence is a naturally loving, healing, and nurturing energy which is always ours to give. Nothing and no one can ever take this from us. No matter what's going on in your life and no matter what difficulties your loved ones are going through, or that you're going through together with them, by giving your complete presence you're allowing the healing energy of mindfulness to shine a light on the situation.

Healing

When wounds are created, healing needs to take place...

You can speak mindfully, listen deeply, and strive to act with love, compassion, and understanding in every situation and despite this get into arguments with loved ones, yell at your kids, get in fights with others, and generally do things you wish you hadn't done.

But that's life, right? We're not perfect, and emotions are powerful stuff. That's just the way it is. Of course, it goes the other way as well. It's not just you, others cause us pain as well. And as a result, we become disappointed, let down, hurt, and oftentimes there's nothing you can do to stop it. So we've done everything we can to improve the quality of our relationships, but what do we do when something still goes wrong?

No matter how hard we try to love and care for those around us, sometimes we hurt them and

Buddhaimonia
ZEN FOR EVERYDAY LIFE

sometimes the other person does something to hurt us. When this happens, you need to heal the wound.

Beginning Anew

Beginning Anew is the practice of reconciliation. When wounds are created, healing needs to take place, and Beginning Anew is the practice of bringing people together to heal these wounds and creating a new beginning based on compassion, understanding, and honesty.

In order to heal these wounds we need to be willing to look at ourselves honestly. It's not always easy to admit that we've done something wrong, and neither is it easy to forgive someone who's wronged us. But our strength is required if we're to heal our relationships and bring them back to a healthy state.

While doing the exercise, both deep listening and mindful speech are to be employed. Whenever one person is talking, the other is to stay quiet, listen deeply, and follow their breath so as to stay calm and grounded. The speaker always speaks mindfully, speaking in a way that they're conscious of the other person's feelings.

The practice of Beginning Anew has four steps:

1. *Water the flower.* The first step in the practice of beginning anew is to show appreciation for the other person. Communicate to them some of the things which you admire and appreciate about them. You'll not only encourage each other's positive qualities, but you'll begin the reconciliation process by showing appreciation towards one another and lightening the mood.

2. *Sharing your regrets.* This is your chance to turn and look at yourself. Take the opportunity to mention aloud to the other person anything you might have done which you feel was wrong to have done and should apologize for. If you both wronged one another, make sure each person takes their turn. Remember not to hold back here, your ability to open up and be honest is depended upon for this exercise to work.

3. *Expressing the hurt.* Now is the time to express how the other person made you feel. Express to them how you felt hurt by their speech or actions. Don't get overly emotional or carried away here, simply express how the other person

made you feel, and then the other person takes their turn and does the same if need be.

4. *Sharing & Supporting.* This is your opportunity to open up and be honest about why you did what you did. Much of the time we cause others pain due to long-term difficulties which we have had long since before a particular altercation, and we must work to correct these over time. Open up and express your difficulties with the other person in order to heal the wound and strengthen the bond between you. If you're the one listening, wait until they're done speaking and then offer your support to them. This part of the exercise will not just complete the healing process, it will often help strengthen the relationship further.

The practice of Beginning Anew is a transformative exercise meant to bring two people together in a moment of healing and reconciliation. Opening up to another person, especially the person who wronged you, is a powerful exercise which has the ability to completely transform emotional wounds, and expressing the positive qualities of the other person helps cultivate appreciation and love for them. We each have strengths and weaknesses, and the practice of Beginning Anew reminds us of this and gives us a way to not only bring these good qualities to the forefront but further work on our weaknesses.

We need to learn how to weather personal storms such as these. Not just within ourselves, but between us and other people as well. Learning how to do this can be nothing short of life-changing. In fact, if a practice such as this was adopted globally it would have the ability to change the world. Happiness depends on peace to exist, but it's difficult to find peace when you have unresolved conflicts with those closest to you. Resolve to change that today and begin anew with those you love.

Buddhaimonia
ZEN FOR EVERYDAY LIFE

Raising

...if you can't help your child stay their naturally peaceful and happy selves, you'll find it difficult to find peace yourself.

Before my first son was born, essentially everything I did was for myself. I was never the most selfish person in the world- I was always willing to lend a hand to a friend in need, I'd help anyone I saw on the street, and in general rarely turned down anyone that asked me for assistance- but every major thing I did in my life was about my own needs and desires. Every day I got up for me, I worked for me, all me, me, me.

But this is the way most of us live our lives, isn't it? Except many of us just never notice it. I know I didn't. I never felt like a selfish person. Sure, I knew people far more selfish than I was, people who would even turn down a so-called friend when asked for help, but still everything I

did was for my own sake. Is this just how it is? And is this OK?

This is our very basic human nature. For hundreds of thousands of years we've been surviving, and so looking out for ourselves is in our very DNA. To some degree, there's nothing wrong with this. We should operate selfishly to a degree in order to maintain our mind and body (at the very least), seek wisdom, and uncover the truth of our everyday lives, without which we're not much good to others. But we *can and should* live much more consciously, more selflessly, in our daily lives in order to cultivate greater peace and harmony between ourselves and the rest of the planet as well as to help improve the well-being of those who lack the basic necessities.

When my first son Malik was born, everything changed. I no longer thought only about myself. I was, as far back as I could remember, for the very first time in my life genuinely concerned about someone else's well-being more than my own. I wanted to do absolutely everything I could to protect my little dude and I was willing to do whatever it took. In many ways, because I had never felt such a feeling of selflessness before- one of the most powerful motivators that exists- he became the fire that brought light to my life. Children aren't the only place we can learn about the power of selflessness,

but few things will compel selflessness out from you like having children will.

We want the best for our children, but as they grow from being tiny babies to flowering young children, you realize that it's not always easy. Children bring a whole new dynamic to life, and communicating with a child and helping them deal with strong emotions can be altogether foreign territory for parents. And as they grow older, if you can't help your child stay their naturally peaceful and happy selves, you'll find it difficult to find peace yourself.

My two boys are crazy, I'm going to come right out and say that in advance. As of writing this, my youngest is just one year old, but he's already standing on the bars of our bedroom bedframe and then letting go so that he can fall back onto the bed- for fun (did I mention our bed is more than 2 feet off the ground?). My oldest is where the difficulties come from though. As I mentioned earlier in the book, he's 3, going on 4, and so he's at a stage where he can be easily mistaken for an adult in a child's body. But this is a common mistake that parents make. At his stage of development, while he's able to carry a relatively normal conversation and do all the typical everyday activities that you and I can do, his brain still hasn't fully developed and therefore isn't the same as a full-grown adult. Why does this matter? Because it means that I

can't talk to him or deal with difficulties that arise from his behavior the same way that I would another adult.

This isn't necessarily true for your child, who may be older, but many aspects of this situation stand true to an adolescent of any age. Your child isn't a full-grown adult, and hasn't yet fully developed, or at least experienced all that you've experienced, and learned all that you've learned. Because of this, you have a lot to give to them. But you need to be careful with *how* you transfer your knowledge and wisdom to them.

For the most part, they'll pick up on your example long before your words, so before anything know that the most important thing you can do for your child is to establish a daily practice and find peace in your own life. That example will eventually rub off on them and can lead to the opportunity to invite them into your practice, even if it's just the occasional meditation session or them learning the power of mindful breathing, which are skills that can serve them for the rest of their lives.

So when thinking about "imparting your wisdom" to your child, throw out any idea that you're just going to be able to talk at them and that they'll listen. Sometimes, especially at younger ages, they will. But the majority of the time they're waiting to see *what you do*, not what you say.

Mindfully Watching

Sometimes, when you don't quite understand what's going on, instead of trying to do a Google search on your own child's behavior (I'm guilty of this too, don't worry...), it can be more beneficial to just sit back and watch them mindfully. That is, watch how they behave, what seems to be going on in their heads, and looking for anything you hadn't noticed before.

Doing this is simple: depending on what's going on, take a seat or stand where you are and observe what they're doing mindfully. Watch their behavior *without making any judgments*. You might feel that you'll need to force yourself to stay out of your own head on this one, being quick to judge your child, but it's better to simply acknowledge any thoughts you notice yourself have and take your child's behavior combined with your reactions as one complete picture of the situation. This will help you discover where the real issue is (yep, because it can often originate with you, not them!). If you can't seem to find an answer after that, *then* consult outside advice. Remember to trust your own intuition, most of us hold much more wisdom within ourselves than we

Buddhaimonia
ZEN FOR EVERYDAY LIFE

actually give ourselves credit for (or we bury it behind a wall of ego).

If you'd like to have a conversation with your child, you can do that too. Ask them questions pertaining to your inquiry and simply sit back and listen deeply to their response, then continue to ask them questions until you're satisfied. Kids usually have no problem answering questions, so it's an easy and often very eye-opening exercise. This exercise also begins to open up the pathways to communication with your child at a young age, altogether critical towards their development and your ability to help them with their issues.

If you don't work now to open up the lines of communication and make it commonplace for them to open up to you about their problems, later on it will be much more difficult (never impossible, though), so getting them used to opening up to you on a regular basis is one of the most powerful things you can do for them. Show them that there's nothing wrong with talking about their problems and you'll equip them with a skill that will serve them their whole lives.

The Breathing Chair

The breathing chair is an exercise I thought up one day when my son was being especially

difficult during timeout. On occasion, I'd sit him down in timeout and, after just a minute or so, he'd begin attempting to get up and run around the room like a nut job. This was pretty common, as he'd generally lose control when he got overly excited. But he started to get worse after some time, eventually to the point where he'd start punching and kicking me thinking he was a superhero or something.

Timeout works great, don't think in any way that I'm putting it down. But to deal with a strong-willed child like my son, timeout takes a lot of effort. So I decided to try something different out, something which would not only make the whole process of calming and disciplining my child easier but also instill a valuable skill in him at an early age- I decided to ask my son to instead sit and breathe for the length of his timeout. This not only preoccupied him, helping keep him from getting up and running around, but it also gradually calmed him down. By the time he was done with his timeout, he was cool as a cucumber, as my wife likes to say. This is a simple technique that can have some really nice results, particularly for an especially high energy or strong-willed child.

The breathing chair is as simple as it sounds: for a length of time determined by their age (1 minute for a 1 year old, 2 minutes for a 2 year old, etc.), they should sit down on a predetermined

"naughty chair" (Super Nanny style) and practice breathing. Once they get old enough you can have them practice actual mindful breathing as well, but simply breathing is a highly beneficial practice in itself when they're around 2 and on. If they get up, they're required to start their breathing over again. When they finish, make sure they say sorry for what they did. You get the idea, typical timeout rules otherwise. The only difference is the fact that they must sit and breathe with you. Yes, with you. I decided not to just make it an exercise where you just had them breathe while watching them, but an exercise where the two of you can come together in a moment of peace.

The breathing chair is a simple and effective exercise- one that even adults could find useful from time to time! Use it sparingly when your child is really worked up, frustrated, or angry to help teach them how to take care of their strong emotions. This practice will be useful to them their entire lives, and will serve them especially well once they're on their own, out from under your wing (except, without the naughty chair...).

The Amulet of Breath

Kids like stories, fantasies, and fairytales about treasure, monsters, and excitement. In fact, we all do, but it's more socially "acceptable" for children to spend their time on these things. Towards this end, I created a little exercise which brings some of that storytelling flavor into the mix and can help create a powerful reminder for any child when they're experiencing a strong emotion or feeling that makes them uncomfortable.

It's called The Amulet of Breath, and the idea is very simple. Create something, or buy something, that can act as a pocket-sized symbol which reminds your child to Go Home and follow their breath when they become angry or frustrated. Your child's amulet of breath can be a small rock you both paint together and decorate, some other small trinket, or a small toy made to look like an amulet or some other treasure. If they're older you'll probably just go the simple route, like using a smooth rock or something else that's "not so weird", but if they're younger I suggest really going all out on this one. Even take the time to create a back story connected to the amulet to make it fun (and make them feel like they're really being given something with some special power).

When your child becomes angry or frustrated, the amulet is in their pocket to remind them to stop to follow their breath. It's a nice little exercise that gives them a constant reminder of the importance of being mindful of their breath from time to time, especially when feeling strong

Buddhaimonia
ZEN FOR EVERYDAY LIFE

emotions. Anytime they feel overwhelmed or uncomfortable, they know that they can take their amulet out and transform that uncomfortable emotion into peace of mind. And this lesson will serve them well for their entire lives.

Anger is a difficult and dangerous emotion for children. But if you take the time to show them how to overcome it, and other strong emotions, you're giving them a gift that will keep on giving for decades to come, so there's few better gifts you can give your child than this.

Something like this, especially early in a child's life, can also help to keep communication open between parent and child. And as I mentioned earlier, open communication between people is powerful beyond measure. Just having someone that loves you whom you can talk to is often all we need to overcome difficult times.

Giving

Never forget the dance.

Giving is life itself. In every moment of life, you're both giving and receiving all at the same time. The essence of life itself is a constant play between giving and receiving, and so to understand this process deeply brings a great level of insight into the nature of reality. And this insight helps keep us grounded and better connects us to the world around us.

May we with all beings realize the emptiness of the three wheels- giver, receiver, and gift.

The above words are chanted by Zen practitioners before every meal to remind them that their meal was not something which they earned, but rather a gift. It's meant to remind them that in every moment they're giving, receiving, as well as the gift in itself. Life is a constant cycle of giving and receiving, and a subtle shift in the way you see the world, from that of the giver and receiver being separate to the giver and receiver being one (and furthermore, the giver, receiver, and gift being one), can change the way you live your life.

It can be very beneficial to take a moment to look around you on a typical day and notice this dance between giving, gift, and receiver. Recognize that in a very real sense your food is a gift, your running water is a gift, the clothes on your back, your heater and air conditioning is a gift, as well as your home is a gift. Whether you realize it or not, these are all gifts. Also take a second to observe all the gifts that you give others. If you work, realize that is a gift you're giving to others and imagine the positive effect you have on people's lives (even the smallest positive effect on just one person). Think of when you give your love and presence to your friends and family, and all the times you've been there for someone during a difficult time. These are all gifts you've given to others.

You might think that working or buying something isn't a gift, but to get money or to give your money is to give a gift as well either from yourself or the other person/people. When you look closely, it's all a play between gift, giver, and receiver.

Buddhaimonia
ZEN FOR EVERYDAY LIFE

The Gift of Life

Giving isn't just the giving of physical gifts though. Those are gifts, but they're just one type of gift which can be given. The most powerful of gifts are the ones you can't feel or touch. They originate from the mind, the big mind, that's aware of its interbeing. In this state of mind, gift, giver, and receiver all come together as one. These gifts are the fabric of life itself. And they're gifts you can give to anyone, anywhere, and at any time throughout your daily life. These are:

- ❀ The gift of your presence
- ❀ The gift of your love
- ❀ The gift of your compassion
- ❀ The gift of your attention
- ❀ The gift of your wisdom
- ❀ The gift of your understanding
- ❀ The gift of your example

To give the gift of your presence is in fact to give yourself, and it is also you yourself receiving the gift of your own presence as well. So in this example you can see clearly how gift, giver, and receiver are one.

Buddhaimonia
ZEN FOR EVERYDAY LIFE

To live in a way that you're constantly reminded of this fact is to bring the whole of the last two sections of *Zen for Everyday Life* together. To live aware of the giver, gift, and receiver being all in one as a constantly shifting dance of relation, we can find greater peace by cultivating gratitude for every little thing we are given in our everyday lives as well as express our appreciation to those around us better by being aware of the many gifts we have to give in every moment, whether or not we have money or power.

Give your presence, give your compassion, give your love, or give your understanding. Whatever you give, give with your whole being. And whatever you receive, receive with gratitude and appreciation. Never forget the dance.

PART IV: Nurturing Peace

Creating a Zen Space

This is your space, a place where all the noise of your life ceases to exist. For as long as you're in this Zen space, you're untouchable.

Eyes closed, you become suddenly alert. A relieving feeling washes over you. You open your eyes and see a soft light gliding down across the room. A loud buzzing rings throughout the room, but you're left unfazed. It's 6 A.M., and your alarm is reminding you to get up for work.

But this isn't like every other day. No, you may have just woken up to a sound you wish you never had to hear again for the rest of your life, but it doesn't bother you all that much. It's Friday, and you're free.

If you've ever worked a traditional schedule, or went to school for that matter, you know the feeling. It's the "Friday effect". You may have just woken up in the same manner as every other day in the week, and you might be about to get ready

for, drive to, and spend the next 8 hours at work, all things you're probably never all that excited to do, but because it's Friday, and you're about to have two full days off, you feel free as a bird.

The holidays have this same effect on many people. I know a lot people who, when the ornaments go up and the smell of pine trees starts to permeate the air, become noticeably happier (I confess to being one of those people).

External circumstances like this can have a powerful effect on our minds and even our bodies. If we can learn how to make use of this power we can emphasize feelings of peace and tranquility in our lives, and, as a result, become more peaceful.

For this purpose, you can create your own personal Zen space. This is a space you can build yourself, no matter how much money or resources you have. This is your space, a place where all the noise of your life ceases to exist. For as long as you're in this Zen space, you're untouchable. Imagine a thin field of energy encompassing you as you enter your Zen space, and as long as you stay in this space, your mind repairs and replenishes itself.

What is your Zen space used for? In your Zen space, you simply sit. This is your time to meditate in silence and solitude. You can simply be mindful of your breath, of the many sounds in and around you, of the sights and scenes within your field of vision, or even do a simple tea meditation like the one mentioned in *Resting*. Whatever you do, be the silent observer of your own infinite nature. Feel your breath, hear the many people, see the many things, and realize the tea as yourself, and you it.

Creating Your Zen Space

So where do you create your Zen space? Ideally, your Zen space should be a room or a section of a room, but your Zen space can be anywhere: a small corner with a pillow to sit and meditate on, a tree in your backyard, or it could even be your car. Or, if you're always on the move, it could be a time of day regardless of where you are. Because you'll meditate while in your Zen space, typically your Zen space will end up being the same place that you practice sitting meditation daily. But there's only one rule in creating a Zen space: it needs to instill in you a sense of peace and tranquility. So as long as it does that, or at least just allows for quiet, it can be wherever you'd like.

This is your chance to replicate the "Friday effect", so use whatever you know will instill a sense of peace in you. For the most part, by simply following your practice you'll eventually develop a strong feeling of peace towards your Zen space, but

Buddhaimonia
ZEN FOR EVERYDAY LIFE

there are a few additional things you can do to improve the quality of your Zen space.

If you set up your Zen space in a room or section of a room, make sure the room or the area is mostly empty so as to reduce distractions and calm the mind. No matter where your Zen space is, you'll want to face in the direction that is least likely to distract you. If you're sitting next to a window and you're following your breath, while at times it can be good to meditate in a more active setting so as to strengthen your concentration, in your Zen space you want pure peace, so turn towards a wall to reduce possible distractions. Lastly, it can help to add symbols to your Zen space like a picture or a trinket that reminds you either to be peaceful or of some other important quality like wisdom, compassion, or love. You could even go so far as to build a small area in your Zen space filled with these symbols, which I'll discuss in the next chapter.

If a time of day is your Zen space, make sure to prioritize the time you spend in your Zen space. Make it the most important thing in the world for those minutes you spend in it, and make any arrangements necessary to make sure you don't miss the time you've set aside for yourself to be in your Zen space.

Being In Your Zen Space

You can stay in your Zen space for however long you'd like. For a general starting point, I'd set at least 10 minutes a day to spend in your Zen space. More is better, but even 10 minutes will greatly help to bring the chaos of the day to rest in your mind and allow you to find your center again. Later, you can spend more time in your space as you feel comfortable.

Do you have to meditate in your Zen space? That's generally the purpose of the space, as the point is to bring peace to your mind, but you don't have to restrict yourself to one form of meditation. If, on a certain day, you feel more stuck than stressed, instead of practicing mindful breathing you can practice mindfulness of your problems. Sit with your problems in mindfulness, simply acknowledging every thought and feeling that arises while sitting. After sitting like this for some time you'll often realize something you hadn't considered or uncover something that was hidden deep within you. This can be a great way to find a resolution to something when you're unsure of what to do.

This is pretty similar to practicing mindful breathing, as you'll become aware of any thoughts and feelings that arise while being mindful of your

Buddhaimonia
ZEN FOR EVERYDAY LIFE

breath, but sitting down with the intention of resolving a problem tends to help me find a resolution much quicker than simply sitting. The idea essentially is that you hold the problem in your mind for a moment before sitting, and this will make your subconscious rest more with the problem than with something else while you sit. Then, you simply sit.

Anytime you need to find peace, go to your Zen space. Your Zen space is your very own Zen temple. Do everything you can to uphold this sacred space, as it nourishes your entire mind and body and positively affects your whole life. Don't attach yourself to your Zen space though. The purpose of your Zen space isn't to come to depend on it as your sole method of calming your mind and healing your pain and suffering. Your Zen space is a supplement to your daily practice, it enhances your practice as a whole. Remember always that your daily practice is your priority and you'll be in the right mind to make use of a Zen space to enhance your practice.

The Ultimate Zen Space

Your Zen space is more than just a physical location where you meditate. The most important Zen space of all is the one within your mind.

Buddhaimonia
ZEN FOR EVERYDAY LIFE

Remember the "Friday effect"? You can create that same effect in your mind whether you're in or out of your Zen space, whether it's Friday or Monday, and whether or not it's the holidays. Live deeply each moment with mindfulness and reverence to unlock the beauty of life and you'll find your Zen space everywhere you go.

Building a Zen Altar

...the purpose of this altar is to help us find our center, remind us of what's most important, and cultivate important qualities to live by.

Zen, and all of Buddhism, has long made use of symbols. Symbols are powerful tools for conjuring feelings and emotions within us, they can help teach us, and they can remind us of things which are important to us.

In Buddhism, practitioners sometimes meditate on the image of a "bodhisattva". A bodhisattva is an awakened being whose mission is to help all other beings become awakened, second only to a Buddha.* These bodhisattvas symbolize important qualities such as love, compassion, or wisdom and help meditators cultivate said virtue. The bodhisattva Manjushri, for instance, is a symbol seen often in Zen. The bodhisattva Manjushri carries a sword which is said to have the ability to cut down the many illusions caused by

Buddhaimonia
ZEN FOR EVERYDAY LIFE

ignorance and wrong perceptions which stand in our way of experiencing the truth. For this reason, Manjushri symbolizes transcendent wisdom. Another bodhisattva, Avalokiteśvara, symbolizes compassion, and is said to be able to hear the cries of the whole world.

But these bodhisattvas aren't gods or historic figures, they're symbols. They're symbols representing the qualities I mentioned above to the highest degree. The visualization and humanization of said virtues into these bodhisattva figures can help us to identify these qualities in ourselves, remind us of their importance, and help us further cultivate them in our lives.

In much the same way that Buddhists have used bodhisattvas as symbols to help cultivate important virtues and remind them of important principles, you can build an altar with symbols which remind you of the important virtues and principles that you'd like to exemplify in your life.

Just as in Zen, this isn't an altar of worship. We don't worship what we place on this altar, the purpose of a Zen altar is to help us find our center, remind us of our interbeing and infinite nature, and then to help us cultivate those important qualities. These symbols help us naturally cultivate feelings of peace, calm, and joy within us and remind us to be mindful, compassionate, loving,

and to live deeply and ever-aware of our interconnectedness.

A Zen altar is a simple place that can ignite a powerful feeling within us. Some examples of objects you can include in your Zen altar are:

- 🌀 Pictures of inspirational figures
- 🌀 Pictures of loved ones
- 🌀 Pictures of nature
- 🌀 Objects which are infused with peaceful or loving memories or some other powerful principle which you'd like to be reminded of. This can be a trinket, a necklace, a flower, or a book for instance.

It doesn't matter what you fill your altar with, as long as the symbols remind you to live your daily life deeply and mindfully and help you conjure feelings of peace, tranquility, clarity, compassion, love, or wisdom within you.

Your Zen altar can be placed in a space as small as a single level of a shelf or bookcase, sit atop a counter, or rest on the floor (as long as you don't have kids, or a dog....or a cat. Definitely not a cat). You can simply arrange your various pictures and symbols however you'd like, so that each is clearly visible and not covering one another. For a

nice touch, if you have children, you can ask them to draw a picture for you and place it up in this area as well.

This altar can be added to your physical Zen space, where you can spend a minute before and after your meditation letting the natural feelings that your symbols conjure within you flow through you and further contemplating their significance. If you have an entire room or section of a room devoted to your Zen space you could even make a large altar, such as an entire bookshelf, and invite family and friends to add their own pictures and symbols.

Taking a moment or two each day to contemplate and meditate on the significance of the items in your Zen altar is a powerful practice which helps remind you of what's truly important in your life.

A bodhisattva can be a real person as well who exemplifies those qualities, but for the topic at hand I'm referring only to those classic Buddhist symbols which are made to represent important virtues.

Growing a Community

...when we come together peacefully as one, everything we do is enhanced.

The principle of the sangha is an integral aspect of Zen and all of Buddhism. A sangha is a group of practitioners who have come together to support one another's practice and live in peace and harmony. To me, it's one of the most beautiful aspects of Buddhist practice and something the rest of the world can learn and benefit a great deal from.

Buddhist monks and nuns understand the incredible power that's generated when people come together. This is how we were built. We're made to communicate and work together as a species in order to live. And so it goes without saying that when we come together peacefully as one, everything we do is enhanced. And this is beautifully displayed when Buddhists come together for group meditation, both in sitting

Buddhaimonia
ZEN FOR EVERYDAY LIFE

meditation and walking meditation. But a community of Buddhist monks and nuns do more than just sitting and walking meditation together, they live together. They live their meditation in every moment, supporting and enhancing each other's practice. They eat together, meditate together, work together, and enjoy each other's presence in every moment.

You can replicate the principle of a sangha, or community of practice, in your own life. But where do you start? How do you begin building a group like this? First, to start, your sangha doesn't need to have any specific number of people. If you and two of your best friends get together once a week to meditate and talk with one another about issues you've been having, that's a community of peace right there. So don't pay any specific mind to building to some certain size, just invite those closest to you to share in your practice. If they do, then great. If not, that's OK too.

So secondly, start with those closest to you. It's important to bring your close friends and immediate family in on your meditation practice so that they can support you and you can support them in their own quest for peace of mind. This can sometimes be easier said than done, but what's most important is just that you reach out and see if they're interested. A family or close group of friends that practices together is 10 times stronger than one that doesn't, so the benefits are worth at least reaching out.

It may though, at least at first, be easier to find a local meditation group. In that case, they're individuals who are already interested in meditation, so they're more likely to be willing to do outside events such as group walking meditation sessions and even mindful adventures (discussed in the next chapter) together. This is a good way to bring your close friends and family in on your practice as well, as some will first require proof that you're serious about your practice before they're willing to support you. Which, by the way, is human nature- so don't knock yourself over it. If you're brave, and your group sessions are going well, you could even put out an ad inviting guests to your meditation sessions. This will take some work, but it can pay off well.

Meditation Nights

The first and most common group practice is a group zazen, or sitting meditation, practice. I'd suggest starting here because it would likely be the easiest to get people to show up to.

A group meditation session can simply be a one hour session of meditation which starts at a designated hour and allows anyone who would like to show up the affordability to begin meditating whenever they decide to arrive and for however long they'd like.

Optionally, after your group meditation session is over you can circle around and have a short group discussion. This can be a time for people to open up about and discuss questions they have with regards to their meditation practice (and you can come together as a group to help try and answer), problems they've been having in their personal lives or at work, or just to talk about anything that's been on their mind. This can help create a new dynamic for the group, bring more value to those that participate, and strengthen the bonds within the group.

From there, you can continue to do a weekly meditation and discussion session as is, or expand it to additional activities like the ones I mentioned earlier in the chapter. I'd suggest having one major weekly or bi-weekly activity that your group is centered around, but however you do it, the most important thing is just that you come together as a group to support one another in finding peace. Everything else is secondary.

A Community of One

What if you have no one? What if your community of practice is a community of 1? That's OK too. If that's the case, I'd suggest taking a moment outside from time to time to contemplate on the interbeing of all human and nonhuman beings. Realize that the highest sangha includes all of these things, not just a few friends. Even when alone, or passing by people as you walk through a street, this can cultivate a great sense of comfort and peace within you and help to strengthen your practice. Actually, whether you have a community of peace or not, this can be a very beneficial practice which you can do alone or as a group.

Buddhaimonia
ZEN FOR EVERYDAY LIFE

Planning Mindful Adventures

A day filled with exploration, beauty, and peace, a mindful day is an opportunity to experience what a life lived completely in mindfulness is like.

I talked earlier about the connection between mindfulness and discovering true freedom. And I briefly mentioned how when we're fully awake to the present moment all boundaries disappear and we realize our true nature. A mindful adventure is an experience in true freedom, as is any moment in mindfulness, but the mindful adventure is about doing things that heighten your awareness and literally compel you to be totally present for this moment. In other words, it's much easier to practice mindfulness during a mindful adventure than it is at any other point in your typical day, so it greatly helps develop your mindfulness. Think of it as the supercharger of mindfulness practices. It's not to be used on a regular basis, but it's a very nourishing exercise that can greatly enhance your practice.

It can take time to develop greater awareness and a reverence for life, but some of the most effective tools I've discovered in establishing new habits for such a practice are simple reminders. That's part of the beauty of a practice such as this. It's so powerful, and it tugs at the deepest reaches of yourself so strongly, that you'll remember it for weeks without even making an effort. And it, in effect, will remind you to be mindful in your everyday life. A mindful adventure therefore, a practice in itself, also acts as one of the best techniques for establishing meditation and deep contemplation as a habit in your daily life.

A mindful adventure can be anything: something extravagant, like a trip to a garden or nature reserve, or something simple like a trip to a farmer's market or grocery store. *What's important is that wherever you go is a place with a high potential for sense stimulation.* This is why a mindful adventure will create such a significant and lasting impression on you- it's not just mindfulness, it's a complete and total awareness of something really, really awesome. A bakery with fresh rolls, donuts (a personal favorite...), and other goodies, a beautiful garden filled with flowers of all shapes and colors, or a peaceful park

with towering trees, lush green plants, and resident wildlife are all good places for a mindful adventure.

There's only two rules for a mindful adventure, and they are:

- ✿ **Go somewhere your senses can run wild.** Somewhere you already enjoy going is fine, but somewhere new can also work nicely because it's a completely new experience.
- ✿ **You have to strive to be mindful for the entirety of the trip,** from the moment you arrive at the location all the way until you leave. That's the whole thing about a mindful adventure- it's an adventure done completely while in a state of higher awareness. If your adventure is a long one, you can strive to be mindful for 30 minute blocks, with 10-15 minutes of break in between.

Staying in mindfulness for a full 30 minutes, an hour, or however long your mindful adventure lasts is essentially impossible, so know that right away. That's why I said to *strive* to be mindful for the entirety of the trip. What matters isn't whether you're actually mindful for the entire trip or not,

Buddhaimonia
ZEN FOR EVERYDAY LIFE

it's whether you put forth your best effort. You could even invite friends and family with you and make this a part of your regular community or group practices, which makes for some nice diversity in activities and can further enhance your mindful adventure.

It's also helpful if you make the conscious effort to put everything in your mind aside before setting out on your mindful adventure. These are all the things that usually roll in and out of your surface-level consciousness, all of your worries and the things you generally choose to house in your mind. Decide to put these things aside for however long your mindful adventure is, and tell yourself that you can pick them back up once you're done. You don't necessarily want to pick your worries back up when you're done, but it's the point of the exercise that's important. By saying that you can think about these things again once you're done you naturally put your mind at ease and make it easier to let go of these things while you're on your adventure.

And if that doesn't work? Make a list, put it in your phone, and lock the phone. This works much the same way as the previous exercise but with increased comfort in the fact that you wrote everything down previously and know that you won't forget about it. Often the real reason you keep mulling certain things around in your mind so much is because you're afraid that if you leave them alone you'll forget them. This solves that.

A Day of Mindfulness

If you want to take this a few steps further, you can make a mindful adventure into a mindful day. A mindful adventure can already be very nourishing, it's a practice which has the ability to literally put a halt to all the craziness of your life and force you to reevaluate your priorities (if you haven't already) in a way that few things can. It revitalizes you, grounds you, and brings you peace. But a mindful day? A regular "mindful day" practice can be nothing short of life-changing. By regular practice I mean designating one day each week or each month to living completely with mindfulness.

A mindful day opens up so many possibilities. You can wake up and practice walking meditation to your kitchen, then prepare and eat your breakfast in mindfulness, do some straightening up, meet your community or a friend for a meditation session or meditate alone, and then go for a mindful adventure somewhere to complete the day. A day filled with exploration, beauty, and peace, a mindful day is an opportunity

to experience what a life lived completely in mindfulness is like.

Crafting a Beautiful Morning

Whatever happened throughout my day, I now felt as if I was more firmly rooted to the ground and less affected by passing storms.

When my oldest son was first born, I began feeling starved for time. The time I was used to having for myself had all but disappeared, never to be seen again. At the time, I was doing a lot of physical training, and regularly meditating before each workout session. I was a night owl growing up, and not knowing any particular reason why not to be, I continued to do so well into my 20s. Because of this I'd often meditate and train from around 10 P.M. to 2 A.M. or so.

But as you might imagine, after my son was born, this wasn't really sustainable. He'd wake up throughout the night, as infants do, and having to wake up to tend to him really cut my already tight

Buddhaimonia
ZEN FOR EVERYDAY LIFE

sleep schedule down to almost nothing. I found myself tired at work, unable to finish my work out sessions, falling asleep during my meditation, and even sometimes nearly dozing off while driving. I had to do something.

Shortly after that I decided to try waking up early in the morning and doing away with my night crawler ways. But what started out as just an idea I figured might improve the quality of both my personal time and my sleep turned into something much greater.

It worked like a charm- sleeping earlier, when the baby slept more soundly, proved to really improve the quality of my sleep. Not only that, the personal time I got was of the highest quality. I wasn't tired, nearly dozing off half the time, and I wasn't tired from a long day. The best of me was given to my morning routine and it paid off handsomely. But something else happened, something far more profound. Correction- a few things happened:

- ✿ I experienced a great sense of peace and tranquility in the quiet of the morning, which had a measurable impact on how I felt for the entire rest of my day as well as helping to advance my meditation practice.

Buddhaimonia
ZEN FOR EVERYDAY LIFE

✿ I became far more productive and was able to work on things with 100% of my focus and no interruptions. This opened up some new opportunities for me.

Each of these things together made the morning into a cornerstone of my day. From that point on I decided I'd never go back. And while the road to becoming an early riser was challenging, the benefits far outweighed the work I had to put in to establish waking up early as a daily habit.

A Beautiful Morning

Within my first year of waking up early, I went from waking up at 7:30 to waking up at 5:00 A.M. After two years, I was waking up at 4 A.M. consistently. And as of today, I'm waking up at 3 A.M. on a daily basis. Once I began waking up at a reasonably early hour, I started to adopt some new morning rituals. After my first year, on any given day my morning usually looked something like this:

1. **Meditate.** My morning zazen practice was always the cornerstone of my day, and at this point I had increased my average session to about 45

minutes every morning. I looked forward to doing this as much as anything else in my day, and the fruits of my practice, although not something I put any focus on, really began to show. I didn't get frustrated so easily anymore, my stress and anxiety had almost completely disappeared, and I felt a perpetual state of peace throughout my day, like I had been controlled by something else all this time and had finally regained control.

2. **Short exercise.** I had now shifted away from my training, but still continued to do short but high intensity training sessions on most mornings. I usually did some version of the "7 minute workout" simply to get my body going for the day and to increase my energy level.

3. **Journal.** I no longer keep a journal, partly because it just wasn't an integral activity in my day and I eventually needed more time to devote to writing, but keeping a daily journal is a really fun and beneficial practice which I did for just short of a year. I would write down all the good things that happened on the previous day (an exercise I originally got from Martin Seligman's *Flourish*), which really helped me to put difficult days in perspective.

4. Read/Write. At this point I had been reading and writing feverishly for some time. Essentially everything I read was on self-realization, life improvement, and the like. All material that helped establish a positive foundation for the rest of my day.

By the time my morning was over, and my only son at the time was waking up, I felt completely recharged, at peace, and ready for the rest of the day. This morning practice, most of all, helped me become more grounded in a very real sense. Whatever happened throughout my day, I now felt as if I was more firmly rooted to the ground and less affected by passing storms.

His Holiness the 14th Dalai Lama (generally just referred to as the Dalai Lama, head of the Gelug school of Tibetan Buddhism), winner of the Nobel Peace Prize and tireless peace advocate, has a similar morning routine. His routine apparently varies depending on his travel schedule, but in general he's an early riser that works consistently to retire to bed as well as wake up early.

He generally starts by rising at 3 A.M. and immediately after taking his morning shower does his morning prostrations (similar to bowing, in Buddhism it's an act of reverence for the teaching

as a whole as well as the act of releasing the ego). Following his morning prostrations, he sits in meditation until around 5 A.M., at which point he goes for a short walk and then eats breakfast, tuning his radio to BBC World News. After breakfast he does his morning prayer and further meditates until as late as 9 A.M.

In no way do you have to wake up early to find peace and happiness, but in my experience of going from one extreme to the other and reading other personal accounts of the same, I've found that an early sleep/wake schedule is more conducive to our natural rhythm. Waking up early and adopting a few daily morning rituals (keep it simple) is the best way you can start off your day. And to have such a powerful practice in the beginning of your day helps establish a basis for peace and tranquility for your entire life. Try it out and be your own judge. Mix and match various morning rituals and try new things out when others get dull (I now do a morning tea meditation, which has become one of my favorite daily activities).

As long as the general idea is there, that is you're waking up early and doing things that nourish your mind and body, you can craft your own beautiful morning that sets your life up for greater peace and happiness.

Buddhaimonia
ZEN FOR EVERYDAY LIFE

PART V: Maintaining Peace

Prioritizing Peace and Happiness

You need to become mindful of what's most important to you in life and shift your priorities to giving the most of yourself to those things.

I think about something often. A Buddhist monk chooses the monastic life (monasticism is full-time dedication to one's spiritual practice, which means to live in a temple as a full time monk or nun). That monk decides that the practice of personal and spiritual growth- both their own practice and the practice of helping others do the same- is the most important thing in their life.

The fact that a monk or nun has nearly all 24 hours in their day to dedicate to nourishing their minds and bodies and to the practice of achieving inner peace is a fact that I'm constantly mindful of when working on myself. As a whole, to be a monk and to live in a monastery practicing for hours

Buddhaimonia
ZEN FOR EVERYDAY LIFE

upon hours on a daily basis and to be around others doing the same is a big difference from someone living a more "normal" or modern life. Living in this way, you're often much more disconnected from people, communicating more over technology now than in person, being subjected to constant distractions and lured into bad habits. As a monk, having such a free schedule, positive environment, and constant support system and guidance is an incredible advantage.

We should all (but often don't) prioritize the achieving and maintaining of peace and happiness. The nourishing of our minds and bodies is the most important thing in life. We want to be at peace and we want our loved ones to be at peace, and if we work to achieve inner peace, continue each day to maintain this state of inner peace, and then show others how to find the same state of peace and happiness, then we'll have a very fulfilling life.

But for someone like myself with all the responsibility that comes from raising a family and putting food on the table, this can be challenging, and therefore at times demoralizing. *But it doesn't have to be.* We're not locked into our current lives, unable to achieve inner peace and happiness because our responsibilities have us seemingly bolted to the ground. This is all illusory, we're not really tied down at all. We can find peace and happiness right here, right now, in our everyday lives. But it doesn't just magically happen...

Directing Energy

It's time to wake up to your life. You need to make your priorities a highly conscious decision.

First, you need to realize that being happy and at peace takes work like anything else in life. But it doesn't so much take extra work on top of what you already do each day, it takes you *redirecting* your energy. We only have a certain amount of energy each day, no matter how well you take care of yourself, and so it's less about hard work and adding more to your life and more about what you do with the energy already given to you each day. You need to structure your life in a way that you nourish your mind and body on a *consistent* basis. If you don't, you'll develop stress, anxiety, and bottle up negative emotions which will affect you for the rest of your life. Happiness won't fall into your lap, you need to prioritize it and place your energy into it.

No matter who you think are the happiest people in the world, they aren't happy because they have something, wear something, look like something, or even because they've accomplished something. They're happy because of their daily practice. Everything in life is temporary, even peace and happiness. This is why we each need to develop a practice which nourishes our minds and bodies on a regular basis, not just temporarily or sporadically. *There is no enlightened state which allows us to permanently be happy and at peace.* We need to be constantly nourishing ourselves. And I don't mean self-improvement, I mean simply *maintaining* the state of peace within yourself.

So you've put a little work in. You've started meditating here and there, but you're getting frustrated. Despite what you know now you catch yourself (or rather, don't catch yourself) going an entire day rushing around doing everything for everyone else (I'm including your ego here as one of those people) and absolutely nothing for yourself. You forget to nourish your mind and body altogether. That can be really frustrating. I know how it feels, I've had many days just like that.

When I first started meditating and practicing mindfulness I'd often forget to practice for the entire length of a day, and really just end up frustrated with myself. But, in this example, meditation is something you really value. You try to meditate everyday as it's helped you to overcome some deep-seated negative emotions and helped you develop a sense of peace you

haven't been able to get any other way. So then, how can you go an entire day and completely forget to do the thing that makes you feel completely rested, happy, and at peace?

It's your priorities. It's the things you do each and every day. This is because your priorities are your energy being directed in a habitual pattern. That's why I often refer to habits and our patterns of behavior as habit energy. It's exactly that- our energy being directed in a specific pattern. It's all energy, and our priorities are our main control center for that energy. Everyone has priorities, but not everyone knows it. And so the most important point to keep in mind is that *if you don't consciously set your priorities then they will be set for you* by some other force, be it the influence of society, your ego attempting to protect itself, or some other habit energy.

I'm not saying quit your job, stop doing certain things that you like to do, or rearrange anything else in your life. But I am saying take a moment to really look at your life and if you find yourself putting too much time into those things that aren't as important to you as being happy and at peace then you need to realign your life with your priorities. It's time to wake up to your life. *You need to make your priorities a highly conscious decision.*

Ultimately, it comes down to this:

Buddhaimonia
ZEN FOR EVERYDAY LIFE

You need to become mindful of what's most important to you in life and shift your priorities (redirect your energy) to giving the most of yourself to those things.

Forget everything else in this book, if you don't do this then you won't ever find peace and happiness. If you don't prioritize it then it will never happen. I'm not saying you have to work your ass off or kill yourself to achieve inner peace, I'm saying you need to consciously decide what's most important to you and simply shift your efforts. We're redirecting, not adding to.

And this goes for your loved ones as well. They won't have the best possible chance at finding peace if you don't commit to finding peace within yourself first. Buddhist monks know the power of this as well as anyone. By living a monastic life they're not only prioritizing the well-being of their minds and bodies, they're prioritizing the well-being of others as well, and every single action they take is in line with what matters most to them. *All* of their energy goes towards that end. And guess what happens? They become the happiest people in the world- Brain scans done on Buddhist monk Matthieu Ricard at the University of Wisconsin have shown that he has the largest capacity for happiness ever recorded. But don't depend on

Buddhaimonia
ZEN FOR EVERYDAY LIFE

university studies for proof, you can experience the difference in your own life by prioritizing your well-being and expressing Zen in your own life.

Happiness is just like anything else in life. So many of us want to be happy, even expect to be happy, and yet do very little about it. And don't worry about being perfect. You don't have to shave your head, wear robes, or become a monk or nun to find peace (that's what *Zen for Everyday Life* is about). But you do have to:

- 🌀 Look at your life, really inspect your daily actions closely
- 🌀 See where you need to make changes
- 🌀 Set new priorities
- 🌀 And take action

And just like I did, even after establishing your practice you'll probably have days where you'll forget your practice altogether and realize you're doing other far less important things with your precious time. And maybe there will be other times where you'll find it hard to focus or break through some frustration you're feeling that day. It's only natural with the average amount of responsibilities we all have living "normal" (non-monk!) lives. But this is perfectly normal, and you'll find peace despite this. Just get back on your

Buddhaimonia
ZEN FOR EVERYDAY LIFE

game and keep at it. The good thing is, you should see positive results quickly which will help to encourage your practice further.

Living Zen isn't about perfection, it's about *life*. It's about making a consistent and continuous effort and making a lot of mistakes in the process. Don't worry about being perfect, in fact don't worry about any sort of result whatsoever (Don't even worry about doing your best- just *do!*), just make a steady and continuous effort and you'll discover the limitless peace and joy of your own everyday life.

Finding, and Redefining, Time

We need to realize the importance of taking time to nourish our minds and bodies and actually make an effort to carve out a consistent time to do so.

Wasting time used to be a serious pet-peeve of mine. If I woke up late in the morning, *look out*, because I was going to take a shot at you. It wasn't quite that intense, but I really disliked waking up late and felt like I had wasted my entire day by doing so. With how early I'd wake up, combined with my kids and work taking up most of the rest of my time, I really wouldn't get much time other than the morning to work on writing and anything else for that matter, so I needed to really make that time as productive as possible. And, of course, that meant that if I woke up late I felt like my life was pretty much over. OK, slight exaggeration.

Buddhaimonia
ZEN FOR EVERYDAY LIFE

Jokes aside, that was pretty difficult to get over. Every day I was reminded of the fact that I hadn't accomplished anything of real value in my life and that I wasn't getting any younger, and now I had the responsibility of raising a child whom I not only had to provide for but who I wanted to be a role model to. I wanted my son to look up at me and think, "My dad is my hero." I wanted to inspire him (now *them* with my second son) to live his best life. So every day that I woke up late I would be frustrated with myself and reminded of that fact.

What helped me get over it was the combined team of mindfulness and contemplating on the meaning and true nature of time. What really is "time to ourselves"? What do we mean when we say we're "taking time for ourselves"? What would happen if I just didn't do anything for the next week? Would anything bad actually happen? After contemplating on time for a while it began to be easier to let go of the whole situation. My desire to hold onto time started to loosen as I realized that most of what was going on was in my head. We're so convinced we have to keep rushing around all the time that we never stop to think that there might be another way, or what would really happen if we slowed down or took some time for ourselves.

Then, mindfulness taught me the true nature of time. It taught me how to have unlimited

time to myself. Mindfulness allows for each and every moment to be a moment of nourishment, not just time off to sit and drink tea, but also when I'm sitting playing cars with my boys or off running errands. Other's time becomes my time as well, and as the lines began to blur, I realized something significant that changed my life forever. But we'll get to that later.

Most people's schedules are some combination of work, family, personal life/family life, errands, and the occasional outing with friends, which doesn't leave a whole lot of time to oneself. But the thing is, when we do get time to ourselves it's likely spent watching TV, spending time online, playing a video game, going out to have a drink, messing around on our phones (probably on social media), and then *very* occasionally something that actually nourishes our mind and brings us peace like sitting down to enjoy a cup of tea in silence.

We need to realize the importance of taking time to nourish our minds and bodies and actually make an effort to carve out a consistent time to do so. Even with my two boys, my wife, my writing, and a whole host of other responsibilities I still have more than enough time to myself. There's really no excuse- you have time, whether you think so or not. You just need to find it.

Buddhaimonia
ZEN FOR EVERYDAY LIFE

Finding Time You Never Knew You Had

I mentioned earlier about how Zen for Everyday Life doesn't require you to make some significant change to your life, and that it's more about transforming what you already do each and every day. Then, in the last chapter I covered another aspect. That is, the fact that it's more about shifting your priorities than it is making some great change to your schedule, or removing things from or adding things to your life. But despite shifting your priorities, you can at times still find it challenging to continue your practice and manage your time and energy. Sometimes things will get in the way no matter how hard you try, sometimes you'll just plain forget to be mindful or live deeply throughout your day because of a combination of how busy you are plus your habitual energy patterns, and still other times you'll feel too tired to do anything.

This is OK. Remember what I said in the last chapter: the point isn't to be perfect, it's simply to make a consistent and continuous effort. That's all that's needed. Over time these occurrences will diminish and you'll become more and more consistent with less and less effort.

Buddhaimonia
ZEN FOR EVERYDAY LIFE

I went through this myself for some time and came up with some solutions to help move my own practice along which I'd like to share with you. These priorities, which you've made the foundation of your life, are the things you've decided are important enough to shape your entire life around. Just as a monk decides to make the practice of inner peace a cornerstone principle of their lives and becomes a monastic to devote themselves to the way, you can prioritize inner peace in your own life.

But you don't have to become a monastic and move to a temple to find peace and happiness. And as we've discussed, in many ways you can do it without changing your schedule or freeing up any extra time at all. The first and most important, and most convenient, way is with the two major skills we used throughout the book so far: mindfulness and contemplation. Of course, we already covered various exercises using these skills, but you getting used to using them in your everyday life and discovering the fact that you have unlimited time because of them is something else entirely.

Everyone's schedule is different, and the practices outlined so far are just the major general practices themselves. You then have to take those and apply them to your own life and schedule. I've found that when it comes to working on myself,

closely examining everything I do during my day and then looking to see where I can fit in "moments of nourishment" on top of what I already do is really effective. But only you know when those times are for you.

For example, remember how I mentioned earlier that I listen to audiobooks in my car? I read a lot as well but mostly articles and blogs online. Most of my book reading is now done via audiobooks and essentially all of my audiobook time is done while I'm driving. You already drive to and from work, run errands, shop, drive to dinner on occasion, and drop your kids off to school if you have any, among other things. Maybe sometimes you do all of these things in a single day. These are all opportunities to feed your mind. I probably average forty-five minutes in my car every day, and through that I read about 2 audiobooks a month. That's just driving, no reading outside the car. You'd be surprised how many books you can read in a year like this.

And remember the other points I covered in Part II with regards to mindfulness:

❀ Walking meditation can be done at any point during your day- walking to and from the store, to and from rooms in your home, and to and from work.

🌀 Stopping to practice mindful breathing is also something you can do at various points in your day- at a stop light in your car, sitting down in a waiting area, or even at your office desk at work.

🌀 And resting- you already go to sleep every night, why not take a moment before bed to practice mindfulness of your body to meditate and improve the quality of your sleep?

Recently, I was waiting in the morning for the local post office to open. Instead of wasting time on my phone, like I would have done in the past, I meditated in my car while I waited. We like to convince ourselves that we don't have time, but if you're honest with yourself and you make the effort to look more closely at your daily habits, you'll find moments in your day you never knew you had. And more importantly...

Redefining Time

When we say that we're "taking time for ourselves", what do we really mean? When we say that we need to take time for ourselves, whether we know it or not, what we're really saying is that we need to rebalance. Rebalancing is the process of regaining some minimal sense of inner peace, the level necessary for us to at least function without

Buddhaimonia
ZEN FOR EVERYDAY LIFE

starting to lose our minds. I've found that understanding this is critical to maintaining inner peace and happiness.

It's never been about freeing, or finding, time but about regaining your mental balance. We think that what we really need is just more time to ourselves. And in some ways, that common misconception is right. We do need time to ourselves, preferably on a daily basis. We can't be perpetually moving, always working, taking care of others, and making plans. But the only reason we need to regain our inner balance is because we're living day to day half-aware, not fully awake to the present moment. To live in this way is to cultivate peace and happiness every moment of your daily life. This is the most important lesson in this entire section.

Mindfulness can be done anytime and anywhere. While driving your car, walking, sitting, cleaning, and working you can practice mindfulness. Taking time to nourish your mind and body is important, but if you can strive to live deeply and mindfully in your everyday life then you'll cultivate peace and joy in every moment, and you'll never lose your balance to begin with. This is the secret to having "unlimited time". Or better yet, how to *transcend* time itself.

Harnessing Motivation

The foundation of your practice must be pure, if it isn't then it's a sign that your motivation is negative and until that changes you'll never be able to find peace.

Self-control is the monitoring of our various thoughts and feelings and the regulating of ourselves based on predetermined goals or intentions. In developing a daily spiritual practice, nothing is more important than this. In fact, self-control is necessary to perform or do anything significant in life. That's why the next two chapters are about developing two aspects of self-control: harnessing motivation and developing self-confidence.

Self-control, or self-regulation, is the entire system which keeps you on course, it's the captain of your ship. The great thing is, nothing does more to help this than the practice of mindfulness and meditation at large.

Buddhaimonia
ZEN FOR EVERYDAY LIFE

But meditation doesn't take care of everything. Mindfulness lets us know how we're doing, it tells us what's going on within us, but it doesn't course-correct us if necessary. And it certainly can't help if you're not being mindful in the first place! Before meditation can do its thing, we need to have the proper motivation. And while meditation does its thing, we need to *maintain* the proper motivation. It doesn't matter how hard you try, you'll never get away from motivation. No matter what you do in every moment, motivation is there as the hidden force propelling you to action. But motivation isn't a bad thing, you just need to understand it and be able to see clearly where your own motivation comes from.

Motivation is the very fuel of our being and it's the reason for our continued pursuit in any endeavor. It's the oftentimes hidden force behind both all mundane as well as extravagant activities. On one end, motivation is simply why we do what we do in each and every moment. One the other, it's a great force which can be wielded to make positive life changes. Learning how to harness motivation is key to getting through tough times, pushing through slow times, and getting off the ground in the beginning of establishing your daily practice.

Peaceful Motivation

Do you know what's motivating you in any given moment? Likely not, nor do you need to, but it is important to know what's motivating you during certain key activities. What's motivating you at work? At play? When you interact with other people? When you look back on the past couple years of your life, what was the major motivating factor? Understanding this is important to helping you understand what's going on inside of you.

Within our lives, we're affected by both positive and negative motivations. Even within spiritual practice, someone can be motivated to find peace and happiness, help others find peace, and overcome certain strong emotions or internal challenges, or they can be motivated to become more productive and efficient so that they can amass power or wealth (often both). This is spiritual materialism, and it's something you should watch out for.

The purpose of a daily practice, such as the one described in *Zen for Everyday Life*, isn't meant to help you become your most effective and efficient self and therefore allow you be your most productive in your business. Although it does do these things, to some regard, and as a plus it can be nice to be aware of, it can't be the real reason you

practice meditation or any of the other techniques described in this book. The foundation of your practice must be pure, if it isn't then it's a sign that your motivation is negative and until that changes you'll never be able to find peace. Your motivation must come from within- not for wealth or power- but for peace, happiness, and to help others do the same. And as we talked about in the first chapter of Part I, *Letting Go*, once you remove the various misconceptions within your mind towards what peace and happiness actually are and how to find them you'll be on the road to naturally purifying your own motivation.

Discovering why you do what you do in each moment can be a powerful insight, one that allows you to immediately change your life for the better. But it's only one of two factors of motivation with regards to finding peace in everyday life. The second is learning how to harness motivation to move towards positive changes in your life, something that at times, and without the right motivation, can be almost impossible to do.

Everyday Motivation

Your daily practice should, oftentimes, be indiscernible from your everyday life. This is because your daily practice *is* your everyday life.

The practice of being peace itself is the practice of living your everyday life in a purposeful, deep, and highly conscious way.

But we're not the same person in every moment. Our emotions, feelings, health, as well as the outside circumstances that affect us fluctuate constantly. Below are a number of techniques which can help navigate the ever-fluctuating emotions and circumstances of everyday life in order to establish greater consistency, overcome daily challenges, and maintain peace:

1. **Tackle small tasks first.** When the day first gets started, have a couple of easy and productive tasks ready to knock out right away. This will motivate you like few things can and is the perfect cure to a slow or challenging day. In this way, you can think of this technique as a "jump start" to your motivation. Motivation is very much like an old train. You need to keep tossing coal into the boiler in order to keep the train going. If you stop, the train stops. On any given day if you can learn how to generate a little energy or confidence you can build on that easily. You can use **the path of progressive accomplishments (described in the next chapter)** to build temporary motivation during a tough day. This exercise is great for

building confidence but it also gives you the motivation to do more. I've used this many times and it works like a charm.

2. **Know why you do what you do, decide what you really want to do, and keep those reasons in front of you every day.** You need to first know why you're doing what you're doing. I'm talking about everything here. Why do you work where you work? Why do you do what you do when you get off of work? Why do you wake up at the time that you do? Why are you working towards that goal? Understanding the underlying motivations in your daily life is necessary if you want to harness motivation as well as if you want to find peace. Once you begin taking hold of your motivation and directing yourself towards a more peaceful and joy-filled life, in the beginning you'll likely need to keep your key motivating factors in front of you constantly. This can be done simply in the mind, or you can place physical or digital reminders in key places if you feel the need. You won't have to keep this up forever, but in the beginning your efforts are fragile and need support, so reminding yourself constantly why you're doing what you're doing helps you to stay on track.

Buddhaimonia
ZEN FOR EVERYDAY LIFE

3. **Don't think so much.** Oftentimes, the more you think the more likely you are to talk yourself out of what you're doing. Especially if it's something you already don't want to do. We can often be our worst enemy, and that's usually because of this inner dialog.

Of course, this is exactly what living your life mindfully is about. Learn to do more while thinking less and you'll find yourself with a keen ability to overcome drops in motivation and energy. Sometimes, if you've been putting something off, you just need to shut your mind off altogether and do it. If you decided previously that something is the right thing to do, but you're having a hard time pushing yourself to do it, then put everything down, stop thinking, and get up and do it. Whatever you're doing, or "need" to do, do it now before your mind can tell you no.

4. **Have fun.** Don't overlook this point. Two people can do the same thing and one will find joy in it while the other will find it boring. And this is simply a matter of effort. That is, making the effort to enjoy what you're doing vs. convincing yourself something is monotonous and boring. Do

this by not taking anything for granted, even the smallest task. Appreciate every little thing in life and enjoy the daily tasks that you wouldn't normally find enjoyable. This is the very essence of *Zen for Everyday Life*.

What does this have to do with motivation? *Finding joy in your work or practice can generate huge amounts of motivation.* In fact, if you love what you do, this can often be all you need.

Buddhaimonia
ZEN FOR EVERYDAY LIFE

Developing Confidence

Within you exists a limitless source of energy.

Self-confidence is something which I was altogether lacking all the way up past high school. Even if a girl walked up to *me* I couldn't bring myself to ask her out. All I ended up doing was falling on my words and losing what little self-confidence I had built up since the last rejection. With regards to self-confidence, there's two things I find interesting. The first is that I really solidified my self-confidence when I began working on myself from the *inside* out, almost altogether ignoring that ever-present fear of what others thought of me. The second being that the most confident people I've found are those sages and wise men whom I've studied and learned from over the years. I've met multi-million dollar a year earning businessmen and women as well as martial artists and MMA fighters of various levels and neither ever came off as cool, confident, and

certain about life as a Thich Nhat Hanh or Eckhart Tolle. This has given me a lot of confidence in my practice.

One of the major ways we often suffer is through uncertainty, both uncertainty in ourselves and uncertainty in our life path. Many of us are too uncertain of ourselves or our direction in life to get anywhere or do anything. This lack of belief in ourselves and in anything else for that matter keeps us frozen in place.

But worse, life itself is always moving and therefore constantly changing. So while we've frozen in place, because the rest of the world is moving without us, we're not staying in the same place. We're slowing falling. Life comes and goes in an instant, and if we aren't taking positive action towards nurturing our well-being then the opposite is occurring- our well-being is slowly degrading.

We don't believe in ourselves or in our life path, we're uncertain of what we want to do in the first place, we're not sure what we're *supposed* to do, we don't think we're good enough, or we don't think we deserve it. These are examples of the many stories we tell ourselves, and it's because of these stories that we live chained to the ground, unable to open our wings and fly.

If we can cultivate true self-confidence, or self-belief, a type of confidence in ourselves that comes from the right place, as opposed to a false sense of confidence due to having money, possessions, or power over people, then we can solidify the foundation of our practice and help ourselves overcome our old habit energies. But that then still begs the question, how do we actually cultivate belief in ourselves?

The Path of Progressive Accomplishments

The Path of Progressive Accomplishments is a simple technique that teaches you the value of simply taking action, however small, and it works as a sort of "spark plug" for the rest of your life. This technique works especially well for overcoming old habit energies. The Path of Progressive Accomplishments is about starting small and moving up gradually. Pick something small like "meditate for 5 minutes", "eat one meal today mindfully", or "have one mindful conversation today". Next, use what we spoke about in *Prioritizing Peace and Happiness*. That is, *prioritize* your goal and make sure you do it. No matter what, make sure to get it done. For best results, do it either immediately or shortly after setting the goal.

What's next? Pick something else and do that thing either the same day or the next. At the very least do one thing each day. If you do that for even the first full week you'll be off to a great start. The important point is that you build up. By that I mean if you're doing one thing each day then tomorrow, if possible, pick something a little harder than what you did today. That won't always be possible, but that's OK. At least pick something of the same level as what you did yesterday whenever possible and build up from there. Maybe then move on to doing two things in order to begin really challenging yourself. Once you begin doing this it might be helpful to start setting reminders in your smartphone or elsewhere.

Action already works as a spark plug for your life, so the way this exercise progressively builds up your confidence level by doing a series of initially small but progressive actions really builds self-belief and quickly gives you the confidence to move onto bigger things.

That's the ultimate point of this exercise- to build your self-belief or self-confidence to the point where you realize that nothing can stand in your way. Nothing is too big. Or rather, that there was no obstacle to begin with. And most importantly, that you're good enough.

Eventually you'll want to move on from the things you started off with, such as "meditate for 5

Buddhaimonia
ZEN FOR EVERYDAY LIFE

minutes", to committing more regularly or heavily to your daily meditation practice so that you can begin to really face your negative self-talk and do it head-on with confidence. It's not meant for you to stay focused on small tasks, even if those do a lot at first to build your confidence.

And remember: whatever it is, when you decide to do it then do it immediately. The more time that goes by the less likely you are to do that thing. The most important lesson of this exercise should be that action really sometimes needs to be taken with an empty mind. If you've previously decided that it's the right thing to do then erase everything from your mind for a moment- literally, just blank out- get up, and start walking, talking, or jumping into whatever it is. Don't let your internal chatter get the best of you on this. Our motivation and confidence wavers, but they're generally at their peak when you first decide to do something, so take advantage of the positive energy and follow Nike on this one: just do it (and do it *now*).

Keep in mind that this exercise is intended to be discarded once you've built up sufficient confidence and broken past your old habit energies. Like anything else in life, don't depend on it as a way of living or it will just end up another vice. Understand what it gives you, appreciate it, make the best use of it that you can, and once

you've built up confidence in yourself and your practice- discard it.

Having Faith

For many, it's faith in something greater than themselves that is the very thing which gives them confidence. But in Buddhism, the word faith is used much differently than in Western religions. The word faith in this case denotes a trust in something's ability which is developed through personal experience with that thing. The first technique of this chapter, The Path of Progressive Accomplishments, was about developing belief in your own abilities. This second technique is about gaining confidence through developing faith in your practice. Buddhist monks, through their own daily practice of introspection and testing of the principles set forth by the Buddha, cultivate a faith-trust in the Buddha's teachings, and this empowers them to continue on in their practice as well as to persist in the face of adversity.

So how does this apply to you? Through your own daily practice, I insist that you test out everything that I've said up to this point. Don't take my word for it on how walking meditation makes you feel, how practicing compassion meditation can improve your relationships, or how building a community of people to practice with you supports and enhances your practice. Test each of these things out for yourself and see what happens. This book isn't about philosophy, I'm not just talking at you, what I'm describing are all things you can experience and test out in your own life. Do so, see the positive effects of your practice, and you'll develop an unshakable sense of faith in the way to peace and happiness.

The path to self-belief and self-confidence is through your very practice in itself. You don't need to look any further than your everyday life to find the strength you need to stand on your own two feet both mentally and emotionally. Find confidence in your breath, find belief in yourself through your interbeing with all living and non-living things, and discover that these barriers are no more than an illusion by realizing that you're a complete expression of life itself.

The Power Plant of Life Energy

Within you exists a limitless source of energy. This energy allows you to take command of your life, overcome old habit energies to establish new positive ones, and do the right thing for the world at large. This energy originates from your spiritual center. But this isn't a place of fantasy,

this spiritual center is an internal locus of control for your entire life. This is your self-control, and it's nourished by your daily practice. Just as a tree passes the nutrients it receives in its trunk up through its branches and into the many leaves that hang from it, by using your practice to go home to yourself in the present moment you have the ability to tap into the essence of life and nourish your mind and body, replenishing your self-control, and therefore further supporting your practice.

Self-control is a limited resource. While you may be disciplined in certain areas, other areas require a lack of discipline in order to provide a place for your mental energy to replenish. The great thing about spiritual practice is, while you work to establish and develop it, flexing and developing your self-control, your very practice can give you a way to replenish it.

This to some degree happens automatically, but unless you monitor it you won't be able to keep yourself on course depending on what you do in your everyday life. You need to stay mindful of the limited resource that is your self-control. Your practice is about dissolving false views, gaining clarity, and ultimately finding peace and happiness, but it's also in a very real sense about providing your mind and body a sort of sustenance. That is, a very necessary food for your

Buddhaimonia
ZEN FOR EVERYDAY LIFE

mind to live and to thrive. This is why I use the word nourish at times, it perfectly describes what your practice is about- nourishing your whole being. This is a point that can't be fully communicated, as words really don't suffice, but when you begin to practice you'll feel the effects firsthand and understand what I mean.

The most important point to keep in mind here is simply to stay mindful of the fact itself. A complete awareness of your well-being as you go about your everyday life will help you notice when you could use a break or a pick-me-up, and during times like these drinking a cup of tea in mindfulness, going for a walk, or simply stopping to practice your breathing can help you to replenish your mental energy.

Kindling the Flame

It will grow little by little, with your own gentle, patient, and continuous effort.

I've always been fascinated with wilderness survival shows, like *Survivorman* and Bear Grylls' *Man vs. Wild.* If, on any particular episode, they were unfortunate enough not to have a fire starter of some sort, because of how important building a fire is to wilderness survival they were inevitably at some point forced to try and build one with nothing but the native materials that existed around them. A challenge even for a survival expert.

First, you have to gather your materials. Hopefully you can find a decent fire starter, which is what will create the spark needed to grow a flame. You need to gather your tinder, which is what will catch the initial spark from your fire starter. Next, you need to gather your kindling which is what will help build your fire. And lastly,

you need to gather wood to maintain the fire once it's built.

Once you have your materials, it's time to build your fire. First, you need to use your fire starter to create a spark that catches fire on your tinder. This can take numerous tries. And just like the survivalist failing repeatedly to create a spark, you're bound to run into obstacles in your own life before building momentum in your practice. But with persistence, your spark will come, it will catch fire, and things will move forward. And when that happens, the world opens up.

Now it's your job to use your kindling and carefully grow the flame. You need to protect the flame from wind, because as it stands any small gust can blow it out. This does happen sometimes, but when it does, you can always create another spark. With your kindling down and your fire beginning to grow, you now need to blow gently on the flame in order to grow it.

Kindling your flame will take time, and it's a delicate and patient process. You can't rush it, and there's no secret technique you can use to speed up the process. There's just you and the flame. As you blow on the flame, you need to make sure not to blow too hard or else you'll end up blowing out your own fire. You need to take it slow, and let it grow a little at a time. It's impossible to give one big gust of wind at your flame and immediately

Buddhaimonia
ZEN FOR EVERYDAY LIFE

create it into a formidable blaze. It just doesn't work that way. It will grow little by little, with your own gentle, patient, and continuous effort. As you can probably tell by now, building a flame, and building a practice which cultivates true peace and happiness in your life, takes your full presence. There's no room for a lack of concentration or a dispersed mind.

Imagine you're building a house, one brick at a time. You need to place the first brick down, spread cement over the top, then place the next brick down, then more cement, and so on. Each brick needs to be placed down evenly and you need to stay absolutely present for the job at hand, otherwise you're liable to place a brick down unevenly and that can mess up the entire foundation. It's a big job, but it's altogether exciting, as each brick that you place down is an action taken by you that affects your entire life. You need to place each brick down with patience and your full attention in order to have a strong enough foundation to weather the storm of everyday life. And if you do place a brick down wrong, don't worry, you can always go back and change it.

If you build your flame with patience and persistence it will grow into a great fire that can withstand any wind. A great flame which envelops everything, and yet stands on its own, you'll have

Buddhaimonia
ZEN FOR EVERYDAY LIFE

realized true depth in your search for peace and happiness.

In life, authentic progress is typically slow and steady. At times, things can seem to happen quickly, but this is usually due to years of hard work which culminates in a seemingly spontaneous surge of growth. This is true not only in business, but in spiritual practice. Don't move too slowly or slack off in your practice, you won't get anywhere like that. Make sure to prioritize *persistence* (especially in the face of challenges) and wake up each day with the same intention: to live in a way that you're fully present with your whole being for each moment that you're alive and able to see deeply into those things which exist in and around you. But also don't go overboard and try to get it all done tomorrow, because it's just not possible. You'll just end hurting your resolve and damaging your self-confidence. Focus on making steady and consistent progress, expect the occasional hiccup (only natural), and before you know it your entire life will have been completely transformed.

Kindle your flame slowly, steadily, with persistence and resolve. Once your flame is built, you won't need anything else. You'll be completely and utterly self-sufficient. You'll become a beacon of light for all those around you. The peace and happiness that exists within your heart will be

impenetrable and spread to all those around you, especially your loved ones. And, provided you maintain your practice, your peace and happiness will continue until the moment the flame of your life burns out.

Buddhaimonia
ZEN FOR EVERYDAY LIFE

Parting Words

The point is to live your entire life deeply and mindfully, not just for a few minutes a day.

I'm grateful that you've come on this journey with me. It was a long one, and we covered a lot of ground, but my goal was to give you the tools to create no less than a revolution in your daily life. Not a simple feel-good read, temporary confidence booster, or closed-minded piece that spoke only to a few types of people and excluded others. I wanted anyone, anywhere, and in any situation to be able to apply the principles in *Zen for Everyday Life*.

And shouldn't that be the point? What's the use with only talking about, say, sitting meditation when others would rather prefer not to sit in meditation for 4-6 hours a day (and not all of us *can*)? Sure, it's an important practice, but if you prefer walking meditation, then make walking your *major* practice. If you're constantly around other people, and like it that way, then find your

center in relating to and communicating with others in a mindful, compassionate, and contemplative manner.

Keep in mind I'm not saying pick and choose though, I'm saying find what fits you best and prioritize that, while still staying mindful of and actively using all the other various ways you can practice. *The point is to live your entire life deeply and mindfully, not just for a few minutes a day.* The great part is, the vast majority of the practices discussed throughout the book can be applied right within your everyday life, and don't require you to make some significant life change. That was important to me in writing *Zen for Everyday Life*. I wanted you to see that real change doesn't require that you make some crazy overhaul to the way that you live your life. Rather it insists that you change the way you *think* and change the way you *look* at what you experience in your daily life. I wanted *Zen for Everyday Life* to show you the way *within* your life as it is now, in other words to complement your life as it is, *not* force you to create a new one (although by all means, go ahead).

And I'm not just saying this because it sounds good, I've used literally *everything* that I've discussed with you throughout *Zen for Everyday Life* in my own life. I'm not perfect, and I won't ever be, but that's OK. I'm constantly working on each and every one of the practices I explained

throughout the book, and you should expect to do the same. All that's necessary is that we make our best effort. If you do that, you'll find peace and happiness.

Buddhaimonia
ZEN FOR EVERYDAY LIFE

Thank You

I wanted to take a second to thank you for reading *Zen for Everyday Life* as well as for supporting me, my family, and Buddhaimonia.com. I put months of hard work into the book and left literally everything on the table to make this happen. I intended this to be my flagship work, and I'm so happy with how it turned out. I hope that the material within *Zen for Everyday Life* has helped bring peace, joy, and meaning to your life just as it has mine.

I also wanted to let you know that I consider you a part of the community at Buddhaimonia, and it's a place where I intend to help others overcome their difficulties, find peace within themselves, cultivate greater meaning in life, and discover how much fun life can be when we learn how to truly let go, so don't let a computer screen make you feel like there's distance between us. I'm right here next to you, ready to help in any way that I can. Feel free to email me directly (here), discuss what's

on your mind in the comments section of my
articles, and let's come together to build this
community into something special.

I want the community at Buddhaimonia to
be a place where people feel they can come to when
they need a friend to speak to, when they need help
making sense of life experiences, when they want
to take their lives higher to a place of greater
wisdom, or just when they want to feel the peace
and joy that exists when people come together as
one. Life isn't always bright and sunny, but if you
know how to live it can be beautiful, peaceful, and
joyous regardless of what's going on around you.
No one person can do it all, nor should they, so I
hope you'll help me in making the community at
Buddhaimonia a place where we can teach people
exactly that.

About Matt Valentine

Author Matt Valentine

Matt Valentine is the founder of Buddhaimonia (Buddhaimonia.com) and a self-published author. He writes weekly on his blog about overcoming difficulties, finding peace, the beauty of letting go, and ultimately how to find great joy in life. General topics include mindfulness, meditation, conscious living, self-mastery, relationships, and simple living. Matt believes that spirituality is simply about learning how to live deeply and in the present moment and that by doing so we can discover the greatest gifts that life can offer.

Matt lives with his wife and two crazy boys in Los Angeles, California. You can learn more about Matt at Buddhaimonia.com/about.

Buddhaimonia
ZEN FOR EVERYDAY LIFE

More from Matt Valentine

The Little Book of Mindfulness:
Going From Stressed and Distracted to Happy and Alive

The Little Book of Mindfulness is the quintessential book on mindfulness, the ancient meditative form practiced for over 2500 years by the Buddha and his long lineage of students, now popular with the new-age technology capital of Silicon Valley, Fortune 500 companies, major medical centers, hospitals, and many classrooms throughout the world.

The Little Book of Mindfulness is literally *filled* with valuable information, tips and tricks, and insights:

1. *The origins of mindfulness*: I go into detail on where mindfulness came from and how it's traveled from ancient India to the offices of Twitter and other Silicon Valley giants, major hospitals and medical centers, and classrooms around the United States.

2. *What mindfulness is*: I explain in simple English how mindfulness works, what it is, what it isn't, and ways to help you make sure you're practicing correctly.

3. *The benefits of practicing mindfulness*: It takes me two full chapters to explain all the reasons you need to start practicing mindfulness.

4. *How to practice mindfulness*: Detailed yet simple and clear instruction on how to actually practice mindfulness in a variety of ways

Buddhaimonia
ZEN FOR EVERYDAY LIFE

5. *How to develop mindfulness*: How to bring mindfulness into your everyday life as a daily practice and habit which nourishes your mind and body and helps you cultivate true peace and happiness.

6. **Plus:** My 11 Best Tips and Tricks for Beginning with Mindfulness and 9 of the Most Frequently Asked Questions on Mindfulness and Meditation

And the best part? *It's 100% FREE* by signing up to the Buddhaimonia newsletter. Just follow this link to sign up and get a copy sent to you now:

Get Free Access to *The Little Book of Mindfulness*

Buddhaimonia.com

I write weekly on my blog Buddhaimonia (buddhaimonia.com) about overcoming difficulties, finding peace, learning how to let go, and ultimately how to find great joy in life. The blog's slogan is the same as the title of the book, *Zen for Everyday Life,* as it perfectly sums up what Buddhaimonia is about. Ultimately, my blog is designed to not only help people find peace but also to show people how to live in a way that every day brings them great joy.

I write a new article every Monday and I'm constantly working on new content and improvements to Buddhaimonia that will help you, so I'd love to see you stop by sometime and check it out. And when you do, let me know what you thought of *Zen for Everyday Life!*

Buddhaimonia
ZEN FOR EVERYDAY LIFE

Distribution

ISBN 978-0-692-37756-7 (DIGITAL)

Buddhaimonia
ZEN FOR EVERYDAY LIFE

Buddhaimonia
ZEN FOR EVERYDAY LIFE

CPSIA information can be obtained at www.ICGtesting.com
Printed in the USA
LVOW06s0324201115

463465LV00020B/269/P